THE WINE MAKERS PRIMER

THE WINEMAKERS PRIMER

PHOTOGRAPHY: CREDIT AND THANKS GOES TO ALL ACKNOWLEDGED PHOTOGRAPHERS, AS WELL AS TO ALL ORGANIZATIONS AND INDIVIDUALS THAT CONTRIBUTED PHOTOGRAPHS TO THIS PUBLICATION.

TCB-Cafe Publishing and Media LLC
PO Box 471706
San Francisco, California 94147
www.TasteTV.com
USA

Copyright © 2016, TCB-Cafe Publishing and Media / TasteTV
ISBN 978-0-9911208-6-4

All rights reserved. No part of this publication may be reproduced, stored in a retrieval system or transmitted in any form or by any means, electronic, mechanical, photocopying, recording or otherwise, without the prior permission of TCB-Cafe Publishing or the Author.

Every effort has been made to ensure the accuracy of the information in this book prior to publication. Neither TCB-Cafe Publishing or TasteTV, nor any of its employees or associates assume any legal liability or responsibility for the accuracy, completeness or usefulness of any information herein, or consequences arising from the use of this book or inclusion in it of photographs submitted by featured organizations, artists, businesses, or individuals. The publisher acts on good faith that photographs provided by featured organizations, artists, businesses, or individuals are authorized for use by the authors and by persons depicted in those photos, and is not liable.

www.TasteTV.com

CHAPTERS

I.	Primer: A Definition	4
II.	Introduction	5
III.	Shauna Rosenblum	6
IV.	Steve Cass	22
V.	Stacy Waldenberg & Linda Baltrusch	34
VI.	Cynthia Cosco	46
VII.	Pietro Buttitta	58
VIII.	Angela Soleno	76
IX.	Joshua Ruiz	94
X.	Jon Affonso	110
XI.	Stacy Vogel	126
XII.	Doug Beckett	136
XIII.	Anthony M Truchard II	150
XIV.	Dan Goldfield	164
XV.	Damian Grindley	176
XVI.	Santiago Achaval	192
XVII.	APPENDIX: Dlynn Proctor	206
XVIII.	INDEX	214

Primer: A Definition

Merriam-Webster: \'pri-mər, chiefly British 'prī-mər\ noun
1. a small book for teaching children to read
2. a small introductory book on a subject

Dictionary.com: /ˈpraimə/ noun
1. an introductory text, such as a school textbook

Wikipedia: A textbook used in primary education to teach the alphabet and other basic subjects. A primer (in this sense usually pronounced /ˈprimər/, sometimes /ˈpraimər/) is a first textbook for teaching of reading, such as an alphabet book or basal reader. The word also is used more broadly to refer to any book that presents the most basic elements of a subject such as the primer "phylogenomics"

Introduction

Our company has long worked with chocolatiers and confectioners. We saw their emphasis on fresh ingredients, unique scents and fragrances, art and design, and the artisan way. Then we realized that they had much in common with winemakers.

Winemaker put emphasis on very much the same types of things. Like artisan chocolatiers, winemakers also have similar challenges. Continually designing new creations, introducing their brand, sourcing the right ingredients, and finding a customer market.

There are many how-to books on starting a business, but often the best advice comes directly from those with actual experience. Thus came the idea for this book; this "primer."

With this concept in mind, we composed a set of key questions and asked them to interesting artisans from around the world with experience in either wine-making, winery ownership, or both.

Their answers on creativity, product, branding and business are very frank and often personal, and written in a journal or diary style.

The information in the resulting primer is worth its weight in gold. We thank each winemaker for their contribution, and share it with you in the following pages.

A.K. Crump
Publisher
TCB Cafe Publishing & Media / TasteTV

Shauna Rosenblum

GENDER: Female

COMPANY NAME: Rock Wall Wine Company

WEBSITE: rockwallwines.com

YEAR COMPANY FORMALLY ESTABLISHED: 2008

Apparently you love wine, what started the love affair?

> It's in my blood. Not literally, but I grew up in my parents winery, Rosenblum Cellars.

How long have you been interested in wine?

> My entire life. Even before I fully understood what wine was... I just knew it was what my parents did. I knew how to read a refractometer by the age of 2. My parents have been teaching me about wine my entire life. It was always presented as an essential part of our life.

Was there anything from history, recent or ancient, that also drew you to the field?

> It is ephemeral art. Our early human ancestors experimented with making wine once they figured out that adding yeast to sugar could make alcohol. There is something quite visceral about reaching back through time and doing what our ancestors did. There is a connection in that experience that is very satisfying.

What was the point of starting your own wine label?

> I have my own ideas about how wine should taste, and even though I learned everything I know about winemaking from my Dad, my style is pretty different than his. When I worked at Rosenblum, I

was following my dad's recipe. That was fantastic and very cool to be a part of, but once I was making the calls on the wines, I got to employ everything I had learned over my entire life but I was able to put my own unique spin on it.

Is wine a luxury item?

Yes and no. It can be... there are very special bottles of wine that carry a crazy price tag, and they are killer wines. Those are special occasion wines. But, my feeling is that everyone should be able to drink wine, every day. In Europe, this is how it is done; most people have one glass of wine with lunch and one glass of wine with dinner. I think we, in America, could learn a lot from the European lifestyle.

How did you go about starting the company from a small business standpoint?

Grassroots, guerilla marketing, beat the pavement, never stop! In 2008 when we started Rock Wall, we said yes to every event that asked us to participate. I personally went to every event with a big smile and a great attitude, and shared my wines and my love for my wines with the various crowds. Capturing contact information became huge, and in 8 years we have collected more than 11,000 email addresses by going to events and if people enjoy the wines, we ask them if they'd like to know more about the winery and our kick ass parties. Hard work does pay off.

What were some of the most important steps?

Having a great attitude about everything.

Find the best fruit you can possibly afford and treat it like it's your baby.

Do everything, and then some to take care of it, and great wine will emerge!

The business world can be maniacal and overwhelming at first, because the niceties of everyday interaction are paired with people's desire to be successful. It can be very disheartening, but you have to remember to maintain your specific focus. Be positive! It is the most important ingredient.

Did you find any aspect of setting up the company to be actually fun?

Oh yes! It is very exciting. Once you finally start to be successful at something you've been gunning for, for years, it is the most incredibly satisfying experience. Also, I was fairly nepotistic and hired many of my friends to work with. That is a mixed bag, but ultimately, it has been great to build something with my family and friends. We all enjoy the wine that much more -- knowing how much freakin' effort actually went in.

What appeals to you about the business?

> It's fun. It is a lot of hard work, but the connection to the land, the agriculture, the people and the artistry of it all is pretty magical.

What inspired the company name?

> We are on a defunct Naval base that is surrounded by a Rock Wall. It is homage to our location.

How did you come up with your logo and labels?

> I have a Master's Degree in Fine Art, and my whole life I have always sketched the SF cityscape. Our view from the winery is the SF cityscape, so it seemed serendipitous to make that our label.

So you've got the business set up and then you have to figure out which products you will sell first. Some winemakers decide this before they even start their company. Which did you do?

> I started out making six wines from eight vineyards. Now, eight years later, I make 32 wines from 63 vineyards. It is sort of a "see what works" sort of scenario. I used to make five different vineyard designate Petite Sirah's, but the market isn't as thirsty for Petite Sirah as other varieties. I LOVE sparkling wine, so I decided to make sparkling wine

for my portfolio, and now sparkling wine is 1/5 of our production. I do a Blanc de Blancs, a rose and a sparkling vineyard designate Rockpile Zinfandel.

How do you go about developing your blends or vintages?

I start with a base wine that I know I want to comprise the majority of my blend, and then I pull samples of 15 or 20 different wines that I think would pair well with the base wine. After hours of experimentation, I have usually rounded it down to the 3 or 4 that I like the best, and then I fiddle with percentages. Vintages are different...for instance, a blend that worked in 2013 didn't taste quite right in 2014, because there were different environmental factors that growing year. I aim for consistency, but the most important factor is to make delicious wine. My dad always said, "You have to make wine you like, because if you can't sell it, you will have to drink it." Even though it is sort of goofy advice, it is very true...so I never put anything in a bottle that I'm not completely in love with.

Where did you learn to develop a vintage?

Trial and error. Period. You can read about it and read about it, but occasionally winemakers experience a torrential downpour in late September, or you hear Cabernet Sauvignon and botrytis in the same sentence, or the sun just never shines quite right that year. These are all things that will affect the fruit. Winemakers have to learn from each vintage and take the tools with them. For instance, in 2011

it was a much cooler growing year than 2010. I had always done co-fermentations with Petite Sirah on two Russian River lots that I do. We harvested the fruit, and I did what I had been doing, but because it had been much cooler that year, the Petite Sirah wasn't nearly as flavorful as it normally was, so I accidentally made these two behemoth wines. They came around after a while, but they weren't the flirty, fruity versions of 2010. Now I know that, and I won't make that mistake again.

What are some key ingredients and tools that you must have?

The best fruit I can afford. My refrigerator is full of various yeast strains. A punch down tool, Macro bins and tanks. A press, a crusher and a pump. A hat, sunscreen, lip-gloss, and a positive attitude.

Do you need someone to help you when you develop a vintage?

Yes. My cellar crew is imperative to our success. It takes a village to raise a wine. I am at the helm making all the decisions on what yeast to use, how many times a day we punch down and pump over, and I taste every single tank and macro bin every day (sometimes 300 macro bins per day), etc... but my cellar guys carry out my wishes and know exactly what a freak show I am about being clean and sanitary in everything we do.

What do you advice people to avoid when developing a wine label or vintage themselves?

Tenacity is important. If you believe in what you're doing, others will too.

So what do you want the buyer to come away with after tasting your creations?

I want them to connect with the wines and be excited.

What are some of your favorite brands of wine?

Rock Wall is my favorite. I also like Williams-Selyem for Pinot. I like Argyle and Domain Carneros for Sparkling wine. I like Bedrock and Carol Shelton for Zins. I love Cabernet from pretty much everyone making Cab out of Napa. Pontet-Canet is one of my fave French producers as well.

Favorite winemaker?

My Dad. He was such a pioneer of urban winemaking... he literally changed the wine world; the way Pollack changed the art world.

Favorite food?

Cheese.

Favorite beer or spirit?

Anything St. George Spirits makes. Particularly the green chile vodka. omg!

Favorite dessert?

Molten lava cake

Favorite movie with wine?

Gotta go with "Sideways." Epic movie.

Favorite book with wine?

The Emperor of Scent

What makes a winemaker different than or similar to other artisans such as chocolatiers, chefs, or fashion designers?

I always compare winemaking to cooking, as you can give two winemakers the same grapes, and the wine will inevitably turn out differently, based on style.

Both are correctly made, but the spirit of the winemaker is always in the bottle, much like the spirit of the chef is in the food.

When it comes to terroir and how it affects the wine, do you consider yourself a floral person, a musk person, a citrus person, a woodsy person, an earthy person, or something else?

I like it all, that is why I make wine from 63 different vineyards. I think there is an appropriate time and place for all wine and all flavor profiles. A 95-degree summer day by the pool doesn't warrant a huge Cabernet Sauvignon, but a nice juicy steak by the fireplace at dinnertime does.

Who is doing exciting things in the winemaking area, in your opinion?

Infinite Monkey Theorem in Denver is doing some very exciting stuff. Sparkling wine in a Red Bull style can, etc...

Are there any developments in the field that you find very exciting?

I find the millennials to be an interesting addition to the wine industry. The industry did not necessarily welcome me with open arms 10 years ago when I bucked tradition on the way almost everything was done. I think we (millennials) like to find our own ways to do things, and we are an experimental crew, so it is sure to be an exciting upcoming decade in the wine industry.

Has the internet helped?

It has been incredible. The addition of social media to our lives has changed the way we disseminate, and the way we digest information. At my family's winery, they were sending information out in the mail. That is a completely defunct way of operating now, and the world of social media has barely been around for 10 years.

Do you have advice for anyone wanting to get in the business?

If you don't like to get dirty, this probably isn't for you.

Do you have any advice on how they can make sure they have a profitable bottom line?

There is no one-way to do it. You can make great wine, but if you can't sell it, then you can't make it. Wineries are considered start-ups for the first 10 years in operation. The overhead associated with wineries is different than every other business. For instance, the fruit we are crushing today will sit

in barrel until for a year before we bottle it, and before we sell it. One has to have a long-term plan in the wine industry.

What about tips for those who just want to drink and taste wine?

You cannot be wrong about wine, which is what is so great about it. If you like it-you're right, and if you don't like it, you're also right. Practice makes perfect-so keep drinking :)

Steve Cass

GENDER: Male

COMPANY NAME: Cass Winery

WEBSITE: casswines.com

YEAR COMPANY FORMALLY ESTABLISHED: 2005

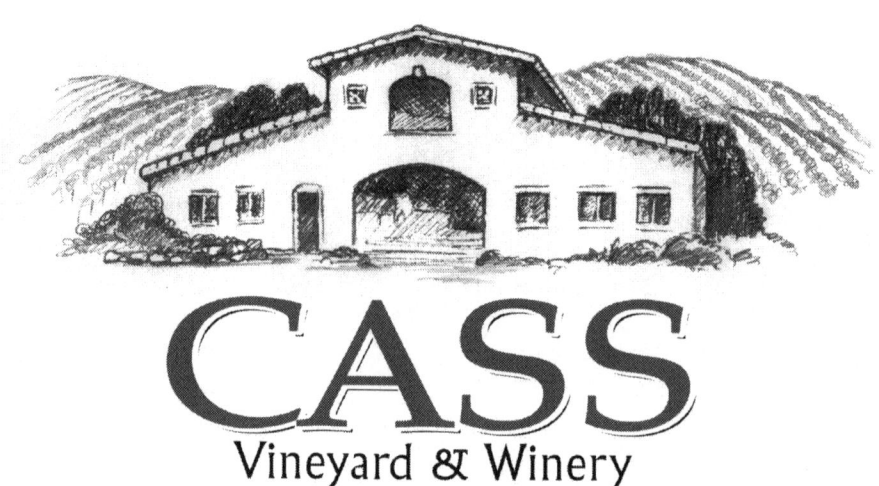

Apparently you love wine, what started the love affair?

> I wouldn't say I love wine...I like wine and I love having my own business, especially a fun business like wine..

How long have you been interested in wine?

> I switched from beer and Scotch to wine about 20 years ago...fewer hangovers, good for your health, goes well with food...what's not to like?

Was there anything from history, recent or ancient, that also drew you to the field?

> The recent studies about the health benefits of wine helped move me.

What was the point of starting your own wine label?

> As mentioned above, I wanted my own business and all l that comes with that I chose the wine business because of the hospitality aspect of selling wines, and chose premium wines because I knew I'd drink my share of the product and didn't want to get into mass production, and all that goes with that...low margins, travel, distribution, large sales teams.

Is wine a luxury item?

> Mine is...

How did you go about starting the company from a small business standpoint?

> We decided in advance we would have a premium product and concentrate on sales direct to consumer, ergo the Tasting Room, wine related events, the wine club and lots and lots of wine festivals.

Did you find any aspect of setting up the company to be actually fun?

> Selling wine should be fun, and it is....recruiting high quality staff and getting to work together as a team eases the pressure to get your business running on all cylinders

What were some of the biggest challenges?

> The investment required to get started
>
> Supporting a large enough staff to provide great customer service

Original Image: Charles Roberts Photography

Original Image: Charles Roberts Photography

Fighting local land use ordinances to provide traditional hospitality services in an area zoned for Agriculture

Obtaining and maintaining the myriad permits required to sell wine

What appeals to you about the business?

The customer and employee interaction

What inspired the company name?

Finding a name that is easy to remember and was available as URL. i.e. my last name CASS

How did you come up with your logo and labels?

Some fun brainstorming meetings with friends and family

Original Image: Charles Roberts Photography

So you've got the business set up and then you have to figure out which products you will sell first. Some winemakers decide this before they even start their company. Which did you do?

> We feel we have one product, premium wine. Our focus was on how to get the wine into the mouths of potential customers...they can't like it if they don't taste it.

How do you go about developing your blends or vintages?

> We decided to go with Rhones as our feature wines cause they grow well in our vineyard, which is on the hot side of Paso Robles. The blending is a combination of what Mother Nature gives us and the palate of our winemakers and partners when we barrel taste.

Where did you learn to develop a vintage?

> We are 100% Estate, so mother natures does a lot to dictate the vintage. In addition, customers tell us which wines characteristics they like with their wallets...we follow their lead.

What are some key ingredients and tools that you must have?

> A very sanitary working environment and good quality equipment...a great barrel washer pays dividends

Do you need someone to help you when you develop a vintage?

> Nope

What do you advise people to avoid when developing a wine label or vintage themselves?

> Know your target market....cute names work in "value wines"...not so much in premium wine sales, price points are critical to success in distribution

So what do you want the buyer to come away with after tasting your creations?

> The wines should all be balanced.

What are some of your favorite brands of wine?

> I prefer wines that have some fruit character, but not over the top.

Favorite winemaker?

> Too many to list...

Favorite food?

> Mexican

Favorite beer or spirit?

> Heffenweisen

Favorite dessert?

> Creme brulée

When it comes to terroir and how it affects the wine, do you consider yourself a floral person, a musk person, a citrus person, a woodsy person, an earthy person, or something else?

> I like the black cherry and other fruity notes we find in our neighborhood

Who is doing exciting things in the winemaking area, in your opinion?

> Lots of experimenting going on, but not sure I am convinced which ones are for marketing and which ones to make measurably better wine.

Are there any developments in the field that you find very exciting?

> Nope..at least not in the last few years

Has the internet helped?

> Absolutely

Do you have advice for anyone wanting to get in the business?

> Making wine is easy, selling is hard.

Do you have any advice on how they can make sure they have a profitable bottom line?

> Start slow and build.

Do you think there are any benefits to private label wines for the winemaker or the private label brand?

Incremental sources of income are always beneficial… the wine business is not a get rich quick business.

What about tips for those who just want to drink and taste wine?

Don't worry about being an expert and try all wines…I can't tell you how many times I've convinced someone to try a wine they previously said they don't like, only to change their opinion

Stacy Waldenberg & Linda Baltrusch

GENDER: Female

COMPANY NAME: Glamma Wine

WEBSITE: glammawine.com

YEAR COMPANY FORMALLY ESTABLISHED: 2013

Apparently you love wine, what started the love affair?

> More than likely it was children and work stress. LOL -- actually we (Stacy, Linda and husbands) did a wine cruise to Sonoma and Napa valley and that truly started our love of wine and on a wonderful wine adventure.

How long have you been interested in wine?

> Over 20 years. Linda and I have lived in different towns and try to visit by phone every week over a glass of wine...or two!

What was the point of starting your own wine label?

> We were frustrated that there were very few fun wine labels (where the wine tasted good) for gifts for our girlfriends and family. All our friends and family love wine and can buy whatever they want for themselves. Wine always makes a great gift. A fun label makes it that much more special to them.

Is wine a luxury item?

> It's a staple in our houses!

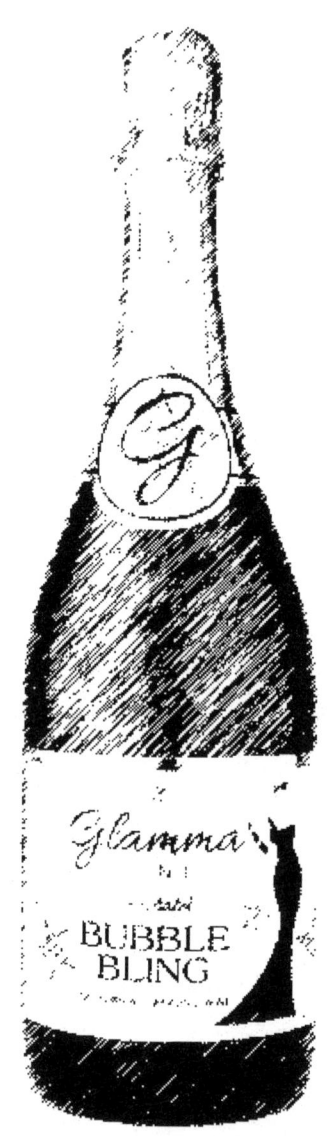

How did you go about starting the company from a small business standpoint?

We both are very fortunate to have very successful family businesses and have saved over the years. So far we are self financing.

What were some of the most important steps?

First step I think was knowing that as family and friends that we could work together too. We didn't want to jeopardize the family relationship in the process. We have been through many family crises together plus have traveled a lot together over the last 35 years and felt pretty confident that we could keep the relationship first and foremost.

What were some of the biggest challenges?

Finding a winemaker who would do a private label wine. We were very fortunate to meet up with Tom Baer and he loved the label as much as we did.

Did you find any aspect of setting up the company to be actually fun?

For the most part it all has been fun. Creating the label and website, going to Solana Cellars in Paso Robles and tasting wine out of the barrel, to putting on wine tastings and meeting everyone who love the wine...not a bad day at the office.

What appeals to you about the business?

> There is so much about the wine process to learn about -- it is very interesting and complicated. Most people don't know, what they don't know, about wine.

What inspired the company name?

> Originally it started out because both Linda and I were new Gramma's. The new term for Gramma is Glamma. But a Glamma can also be a fun gal who loves her bling and glamour. We had so many young gals say "I'm a Glamma too" that we really haven't focused on the Gramma aspect. It appeals to all ages of Glamma's!

How did you come up with your logo and labels?

> We worked with an agency, told them what we wanted and they did an amazing job.

So you've got the business set up and then you have to figure out which products you will sell first. Some winemakers decide this before they even start their company. Which did you do?

> While working with Tom the winemaker, we decided right at the beginning that we would start with the 4 wines; Cabernet Sauvignon, Viognier, Chardonnay and a Sparkling Wine that we call "Bubble Bling." We thought those wines would appeal to a broad base of people.

How did you go about developing your blends or vintages?

> When our wines are pressed and barreled up, we separate our fermented free run juice from our pressed wine; we use twenty to twenty five percent new French or American oak barrels and the balance of the wine is placed in neutral oak barrels that have then been aged for fourteen to twenty four months. Starting with a neutral single free run varietal, we cross blend small percentages of the pressed and new oaked wine in to rows of wine glasses forming a grid in stepped ratios, we also blend prior bench mark percentages from earlier vintages, this all performed in a blind tasting, usually with trusted colleagues and friends! We look for the glass showing the best characteristics of that varietal. We would perform the same processes for a Meritage blend as well.

Where did you learn to develop a vintage?

Working with other accomplished winemakers and vineyard owners in the Paso Robles and California Central Coast area.

What are some key ingredients and tools that you must have?

Quality grapes, yeast, acid, and enzymes.

Do you need someone to help you when you develop a vintage?

Yes we get seasonal help from family, friends and colleagues.

What do you advise people to avoid when developing a wine label or vintage themselves?

> Profitability is based upon both the label and vintage, both need to fit your market demographic. It's a study. You HAVE to love it, and live it!

> Last of all, Marketing. The global market is always shifting, keeping up with technology and maintaining an intense focus on your brand value.

So what do you want the buyer to come away with after tastings your creations?

> An enjoyable, memorable experience, with the consumer building an interest in a long term relationship with the brand.

What are some of your favorite brands of wine?

> Saxum, Linne Calodo, Eberle,

Favorite winemaker?

> Tom Baer of course.

Favorite food?

ALL

Favorite beer or spirit?

Not fans of beer.

Favorite dessert?

Would rather have appetizers – no dessert.

Favorite movie with wine?

> ALL

Favorite book with wine?

> ALL

What makes a winemaker different than or similar to other artisans such as chocolatiers, chefs, or fashion designers?

> We're splitting hairs when we try to make comparisons from different professions. Wine making like all those mentioned develops and evolves over time, education, internship, mentoring relationships, books and the vast array of information on line, and anyone can make wine and follow the simple recipes. It's how you manage each ingredient and a personal commitment to your art that makes fine wine.

When it comes to terroir and how it affects the wine, do you consider yourself a floral person, a musk person, a citrus person, a woodsy person, an earthy person, or something else?

> By owning an Estate vineyard in Paso Robles AVA, the topic of terroir run all over the county, generally I would say I'm all of the above, all of those elements are a part of wine making. Starting in the vineyard through harvest; winemaking production, cellar work, and blending all provide and contribute to these profiles.

Who is doing exciting things in the winemaking area, in your opinion?

There are a lot of small label wineries that are starting to develop distilling programs, culling out wines that don't meet there standards and are making wine Vodka and Gin.

Are there any developments in the field that you find very exciting?

Flash Détente method of extraction.

Has the internet helped?

Yes – Facebook, Instagram and our website (www.glammawine.com) has helped get our brand out there.

Do you have advice for anyone wanting to get in the business?

Do your homework, make sure distributors have room for more wines, check into all the state laws regarding alcohol, some state allow direct importing to a retail store with an alcohol license – others don't.

Do you have any advice on how they can make sure they have a profitable bottom line?

Talk with distributors and store owners about what price point they are willing to buy at.

Do you think there are any benefits to private label wines for the winemaker?

> Yes!

What about tips for those who just want to drink and taste wine?

> JUST DO IT! You will learn so much by trying and tasting many different wines. And enjoy the journey.

Cynthia Cosco

GENDER: Female

COMPANY NAME: Passaggio Wines

WEBSITE: passaggiowines.com

YEAR COMPANY FORMALLY ESTABLISHED: 2008

Apparently you love wine, what started the love affair?

I was raised with wine. My Italian grandfather made wine in the basement

How long have you been interested in wine?

Since I can remember

Was there anything from history, recent or ancient, that also drew you to the field?

Just passion

What was the point of starting your own wine label?

I wanted to create a community that loves to gather around the table with wonderful friends, great food, and awesome wines.

Is wine a luxury item?

I believe wine is an everyday item

How did you go about starting the company from a small business standpoint?

You get a plan, work the plan, rely on others for help, and watch it succeed.

What were some of the most important steps?

Creating a brand that people will understand

What were some of the biggest challenges?

Marketing

Did you find any aspect of setting up the company to be actually fun?

Setting up the wine club

What appeals to you about the business?

The wine industry community

What inspired the company name?

Passaggio means "passage way" in Italian. It's a tribute to my great grandfather who came to the US from Italy

How did you come up with your logo and labels?

It was a long process. I wanted something that meant journey or passage. The label has progressed over the years. I am finally very happy with it.

So you've got the business set up and then you have to figure out which products you will sell first. Some winemakers decide this before they even start their company. Which did you do?

I knew right away which varietal I wanted to make before I actually got the business off the ground. I actually started Passaggio Wines with only 50 cases of unoaked Chardonnay.

How do you go about developing your blends or vintages?

I like to watch the trends. Vintages speak for themselves. We, as winemakers, make the best of what mother nature gives us. Blends are another story. That's the fun part of winemaking. Make what you think is fun. Blends are a big trend right now.

Where did you learn to develop a vintage?

I worked for Chateau St Jean and a huge custom crush facility for over 7 years. I saw all sorts of styles of winemaking.

What are some key ingredients and tools that you must have?

Great grapes, and a good palate, and a passion for what you are doing.

Do you need someone to help you when you develop a vintage?

It's always good to have people around that can help me with heavy lifting...LOL

What do you advise people to avoid when developing a wine label or vintage themselves?

Start off slow...with a few barrels. See how it goes and then build your brand from there. Have a solid business plan and marketing plan

So what do you want the buyer to come away with after tastings your creations?

I want the buyer to want to purchase more of course. I want them to be interested enough to read about my story and how I got here today. I want them to be intrigued enough to pair the wine with food and share it with friends.

What are some of your favorite brands of wine?

I tend to gravitate to the smaller producers. I love MacLaren Syrahs, Bedrock Zins, and Twomey Sauv Blanc.

Favorite winemaker?

Linda Trotta

Favorite food?

Grilled Salmon

Favorite beer or spirit?

Great White Lost Coast Brewery

Favorite dessert?

Red Velvet Cake

Favorite movie with wine?

There are so many movies out there I really don't have a favorite one, but I love to relax in front of the TV with great glass of wine.

Favorite book with wine?

Again, I really don't have a favorite book, but sitting with a good book and a glass of wine by the fireplace is one of my favorite ways to relax.

What makes a winemaker different than or similar to other artisans such as chocolatiers, chefs, or fashion designers?

I believe we are most similar in our passion for what we do

When it comes to terroir and how it affects the wine, do you consider yourself a floral person, a musk person, a citrus person, a woodsy person, an earthy person, or something else?

I try to let the terroir speak for itself. I would consider myself all the above

Who is doing exciting things in the winemaking area, in your opinion?

That's the million dollar question. There are so many small producers doing great things in the Napa/Sonoma area.

Are there any developments in the field that you find very exciting?

Cold stability is always fascinating to me. There are new products on the market that help aid in this without using glycol jacketed tanks.

Has the internet helped?

Of course. It helps with everything LOL

Do you have advice for anyone wanting to get in the business?

Start slow, have a plan and stick to it. Surround yourself with people who are experts in what they do in the industry. Make great wine. Market yourself well.

Do you have any advice on how they can make sure they have a profitable bottom line?

Have a very tight budget

Do you think there are any benefits to private label wines for the winemaker or the private label brand?

Private labels are fun and give the person a way of sharing their passion with others.

What about tips for those who just want to drink and taste wine?

I say drink what you like but continue to expand your pallet. It's all about wonderful friends, great food, and awesome wines...

Pietro Buttitta

GENDER: Male

COMPANY NAME: Prima Materia and Rosa d'Oro Vineyards

WEBSITE: Prima-materia.co & Rosadorovineyards.com

YEAR COMPANY FORMALLY ESTABLISHED: Rosa d'Oro 2001, Prima Materia 2015

Apparently you love wine, what started the love affair?

I grew up on a bulk wine vineyard in the Russian River Valley in the 70's when grapes were as valuable as prunes or pears, maybe less. So I have an ingrained vineyard love. I am a chef and restaurant consultant as well, so later in life as my cooking and tasting skills grew, wine was part of that.

How long have you been interested in wine?

I have been intensely interested in wine since 2007. I went from a chef gig to working at a wine shop, helping out on a vineyard and then full time viticulture and winemaking – plus all the marketing, packaging, and business stuff that goes along with growing a brand.

Was there anything from history, recent or ancient, that also drew you to the field?

Wine is very historical which is important to me, but also a potential sticking point with tremendous orthodoxy and ideological baggage. For me wine is like a simple Italian dish – the componentry is simple but the devil is in all the details. Wine history is very much part of its appeal, and I hate modern Costco-style wine for that reason when it is just a soulless commodity on a shelf.

What was the point of starting your own wine label?

> I joined a preexisting brand in 2008 but retooled, redesigned, and had a lot to do with branding and marketing, so that felt partially mine. 2011 was the first year of my own small label. That created the blue print for Prima Materia which is my baby.

Is wine a luxury item?

> This is a complicated question. Wine has always been both – magical as a luxury item like Falernian wine 2,000 years ago but important for decent daily life at the same time. Wine is a food stuff. There is basic rice, then really good rice. Decent chicken then really, really good chicken which is more effort and more demanding to produce. Anything "artisanal" is edging toward luxury, but this shouldn't necessarily be a bad word. But, there are bad and vapid luxury wines, just like people. Certainly all the "wine culture" Napa Valley type stuff is obnoxious, but I am come at this from a farmer/cook's perspective, not a luxury consumer's perspective.

How did you go about starting the company from a small business standpoint?

I am still struggling with this. I am a farmer from a poor family, but I need to find financial partners to help in what is considered a vanity business and run as lean and responsible business based on good decision making and entrepreneurial principles. Right now I am begging for money. That is how you start if you have skills but no personal or family money.

What were some of the most important steps?

Grow the grapes right, detail in the vineyard, sanitation, responsibility and constant engagement in the winery. Find and listen to your inner intuition. I was a chef first so this wasn't too hard as I already trusted my own palate. Learning about global wine and what the grapes can do in different places is extremely important to my wine model as well. Then there is all of the business stuff, which is a long learning process too.

What were some of the biggest challenges?

I specialize in non-mainstream grapes, Aglianico, Nebbiolo, Carmenere, Montepulciano, etc., so there is already a limited market. This needs to be used in creative ways to become an advantage. The business side is the hardest. Grapes and wine are the zen part of challenge. The business side will kill you if you make a mistake.

Did you find any aspect of setting up the company to be actually fun?

Learning about business is kind of cool, a lot like a second language with its peculiar inchoate logic.

What appeals to you about the business?

I am completely a food and wine guy. Years spent in kitchens, an executive chef and I am a restaurant consultant. I also teach wine seminars, and have led some on both regions and wine history. The vineyard is my favorite place, the winery second, behind a stove third. That is appealing and I will still be learning to the very end.

What inspired the company name?

Prima Materia is part of the alchemy theme that evolved naturally. It just works with my balancing wine and food and hopefully creating higher forms. I was a philosophy student and also appreciate the bizarre exploratory nature of the alchemical field and provisional methods of reason. Plus the imagery is really cool and interesting.

How did you come up with your logo and labels?

The first year I produced the Trigrammaton wine my girlfriend helped produce an image of two dragons made of grapevines balancing each other, struggling but rooted and solid. This had personal meaning as well as strong metaphorical and literal ties to the vineyard and human aspects of wine making. We are now delving into different alchemical concepts for each label. At Rosa d'Oro Vineyards the imagery was related to each varietal in some specific way.

So you've got the business set up and then you have to figure out which products you will sell first. Some winemakers decide this before they even start their company. Which did you do?

Oh yeah, if you are a craftsperson you need to produce something that you are personally invested in. I love Aglianico, so I will always produce one. If you just want to produce a generic wine, like an oaky Zinfandel, then you justify the market first and create a product for the market. You say Cabernet sells, so you make Cabernet. I will always chose the first model.

How do you go about developing your blends or vintages?

This is where things start becoming personal and sensitive or creative. Intuiting a vintage is important. You will generally have an idea of what it will be like from the growing conditions and what the grapes are telling you. But then it gets into knowing when to intervene or step out of the way. Was it a cold year and the wines seem light? Do you fix this or get in tune with it and help it sing? These are serious decisions. Each year will say something different, even from the same vineyard block. Blending is a good resource but small wineries don't have lots of blending components lying around, so that is limited usually. Blending is an art. I like the purity of varietals but the difference between 3% and 5% can destroy or build something great. I am used to having vineyard control so I work to create either complexity in the vineyard (shading, crop load) or focus (uniformity) in the vineyard and then in the winery by breaking lots into different fermentation styles and recombining.

Where did you learn to develop a vintage?

Unfortunately I never had anyone to teach me, it is intuitive and iterative and comes from listening originally. Often it doesn't even come into focus until a year later.

What are some key ingredients and tools that you must have?

> My tools have been low tech with lots of shoveling and comparatively low tech equivalent. Fancy tanks, concrete fermenters and new oak barrels are far beyond the Rosa d'Oro budget and my own at this time. Vineyard control is the key ingredient. Tools are almost unimportant beyond something to hold grapes in, a pump and a hose and something to age it in.

Do you need someone to help you when you develop a vintage?

> No, although it is helpful to hear what others are experiencing, usually as confirmation.

What do you advise people to avoid when developing a wine label or vintage themselves?

> Everyone has advice. People who never buy your wine will tell you it should be more expensive. People who do buy it want it cheaper. One person hates the label and the next loves it. I have watched people drink straight vinegar and fall in love with it. On one hand you should listen to the market and opinions. On the other hand you need to shut everything out and make choices. Avoid the romantic stuff and be realistic. If you only make 500 cases and want to sell it yourself,

stop thinking about how the bottle looks on a grocery store shelf. Avoid being the same as everyone else, until you can be better than everyone else. Barrels are not magical – they are microbial nightmares. Listen constantly to the wine. Avoid making it something it isn't.

So what do you want the buyer to come away with after tastings your creations?

It should be enjoyable of course, but it should be interesting or engaging. I would like my Nebbiolo to make you go try others from Italy or here. Ideally it should have a place in the wine world and spark more interest in it. It is not just a commodity.

What are some of your favorite brands of wine?

I'm a grapes guy, not a winery guy. My first real wine moment though was a Marchesi di Gresy tasting, so I will always be attached to those moments. Things like Corison cabernet, great Burgundy, are always worth hunting down.

Favorite winemaker?

People like Paolo Bea motivate me everyday, even when I am cooking.

Favorite food?

Too many to say. Like many modern chefs I love everything from SouthEast Asian, French bistro to Italian cheeses. I love working with fish. The Prima Materia winery will include a weekly supper club. I will recreate everything from Roman feasts to William Burrough's Interzone as a conceptual dinner and everything in between. I guess my comfort foods are Vietnamese noodle bowls, a good oniony gyro, well made pasta and good French cheese.

Favorite beer or spirit?

Tough one. I love citrus bitter flavors so a Negroni always hits the spot. I'm not a modern overhopped beer fan so I enjoy ambers, nitro stouts and heavy ales.

Favorite dessert?

I like simple dessert. Uncooked fruits, pistachios and citrus, high quality chocolate from different terroirs. I do have a sweet tooth and was a pastry chef for a year so I have a strong appreciation of a well-made dessert.

Favorite movie with wine?

> Eh, wine movies are bad. It just is not an item for movie making. I did like Mondovino. Somm made me gag and was unwatchable, and I am a level 2 sommelier and constantly fighting with myself whether to pursue advanced or not. I'll plug A Matter of Taste on Paul Liebrandt as tangentially related (food) and pretty on point.

Favorite book with wine?

> I read cookbooks — what do you expect from a chef? With wine right now I am still digesting Relae and Alexandre Gauthiere's cookbook. There is a deeper meaning to a good cookbook (or good chef) after the initial, surface effect. It can take years and years. Wine can help with that second order significance.

What makes a winemaker different than or similar to other artisans such as chocolatiers, chefs, or fashion designers?

> Chefs work harder, have better business minds and do way more than winemakers who are generally lazy, over-privileged and whiny in California. There are many exceptions of course. For me wine is the zen side, the side teaching me patience ompared to the speed and frenzy of cooking which is the active, pivoting, warp

speed metal-driven surface passion part. They create a whole. So winemakers are a little similar to chefs in reversed form with little time pressure, low activity and a much quieter discipline to me. I need both.

When it comes to terroir and how it affects the wine, do you consider yourself a floral person, a musk person, a citrus person, a woodsy person, an earthy person, or something else?

All of them. Each grape has a different internal expression and form to be discovered. All of those things are beautiful and of great value. There is no preference for one over the other, though I am a closet Alto Adige Pinot Blanc drinker, putting me on the floral side. But I love stinky grapes (except Pinotage) too.

Who is doing exciting things in the winemaking area, in your opinion?

There are many hipster winemakers doing cool things that I grudgingly like. Jon Bonné builds their businesses for them, just like Robert Parker. I won't name names but that makes it obvious. I am glad to see winemakers stepping back, laying off oak and going less ripe when appropriate. Unfortunately doing some cool things means really expensive equipment sometimes, like concrete tanks. Pricey yuppie equipment shouldn't equal exciting wine but interesting things do come out of these rediscovered formats. In Lake County there is hardly any interesting winemaking – it is all very orthodox standard stuff, even if some is very good. Some second-generation winemakers are doing interesting refinement things and delving into terroir that should be commended.

Are there any developments in the field that you find very exciting?

We are only beginning to map the microbial soup of wine. Rootstocks are nearly totally ignored and are a super important undiscovered country. Certainly I get excited when more new grapes come in. I would plant Valpolicella in Green Valley and Baga in Baja if I had my way. These are exciting for me.

Has the internet helped?

Too much information is just right for me, so I do enjoy the access. Marketing wine online is still a developing discipline, despite all the myths the marketers and sales peoples spin. Wine is so experiential that it really just does not match the internet easily.

Do you have advice for anyone wanting to get in the business?

> Listen, learn, start in the vineyard. Bonus points if you are a professional cook or gourmand. But, making wine is a business and at the end of the day you could still go out of business making the best wine on earth. Develop your palate, control the environment and interact with the wine constantly. My biggest lesson is always learning patience and listening. At some point stop doing and just listen.

Do you have any advice on how they can make sure they have a profitable bottom line?

> I am still figuring this part out myself. Like a restaurant a winery can nickel and dime you to death.

Do you think there are any benefits to private label wines for the winemaker or the private label brand?

> I avoid making shiners and would never put my label on someone else's wine unless it was absolutely necessary, like short production for a first-year brand. People who put their names on grapes they didn't grow or wine they didn't make are dicks.

What about tips for those who just want to drink and taste wine?

For people who just want to enjoy I say drink globally and explore. Don't let Bevmo or Total Wine limit your world with their corporate brands. Find a small trustworthy wine shop, or use the interent. Explore Italy, Spain and France. Then go German and Greek. Learn the language, walk some vineyards and explore. Wine is an agricultural product, get your feet dirty now and then. Famiarize yourself with your own palate, then push those boundaries and ask why? Then work food into the equation. Then keep going.

Angela Soleno

GENDER: Female

COMPANY NAME: Turiya Wines

WEBSITE: turiyawines.com

YEAR COMPANY FORMALLY ESTABLISHED: 2008

Apparently you love wine, what started the love affair?

Ah, what a question... I had a breakup that drove me to drink; Actually, as I was taking a vacation to recover from a broken heart, I found comfort in a bottle of Chianti. It warmed me up, put a smile on my face and captivated me. It was such a strong connection that I remember thinking I've found love again. It has proven to be true!

How long have you been interested in wine?

2006 was when I had the glass that inspired me to change careers.

Was there anything from history, recent or ancient, that also drew you to the field?

I am always inspired by current events. I was inspired to remain a small, focused producer when I witnessed the economic collapse in 2008; it was a lesson in history that I still use. Feminism is also a strong current that inspires me to stand up for doing what you love, no matter the gender typically associated with it.

What was the point of starting your own wine label?

I started Turiya for several reasons; the word means to be aware. Fully conscience. I aspire to be aware; educated, realistic, and truthful. My

direct connection with the entire business (as it is solely operated by myself), gives me the ability to be all of those things. I want to create and continue to pass on this 'awareness'. I love that consumers ARE educating themselves about the things we put in our bodies, from the eggs we buy to the vaccinations we have for so long taken without question. I also wanted some wines made to my liking. I prefer aged wines. I prefer soft, nuanced, layered wines that are a very natural reflection of the earth from which they came and the berry that it is. I wanted to produce these Old World style wines in California; specifically on the Central Coast where I grew up.

Is wine a luxury item?

Absolutely.

How did you go about starting the company from a small business standpoint?

I begged and borrowed. Well, kind of. Fortunately I grew up here on the Central Coast, I formed alliances with other wine producers before jumping in. I am small. I started with 2 tons of grapes that I sourced from a local vineyard. I outsourced the big equipment like the crusher de-stemmer and press, I rented space from another wine producer. When it came to bottling it was and still is all done by hand. Luckily wine takes a few years before it *is ready to sell and during that time I was able to work, put my money into my business and focus on building my various business tools such as my website, the label design, technical sheets, open bank accounts, file forms and all that fun stuff.*

What were some of the most important steps ?

The most important step was to build a strong business model then to take the leap.

What were some of the biggest challenges?

The biggest challenge is probably standing out. There are over 4,000 California wineries and over 8,000 nationally; I remember just trying to create a buzz, the word of mouth phenomena, and industry recognition. Turiya is an uber small label, I don't have a tasting room open to the public, I don't submit the wines for reviews, I don't distribute, nor do I have a wine club, and you have to get on an allocation list to get the password for my wine-shop. Even though it may sound like I have done everything possible to NOT sell a bottle of wine, I have done the opposite. I am set apart. I reach consumers directly and make real connections, but I don't want to give away all my secrets...

Another industry challenge is educating or re-educating the consumer about wine economics. I feel the industry has been cheapened by the recession of 2008; small producers were really hurt during that time, many closing shop for good, and others discounting the heck out of the wines to move them into someone's home and take the liability of the wine going bad off their minds. Sadly the wave of discounts left consumers a new opinion that wineries can afford to discount wine; so selling this high-end, luxury product is harder than ever if we don't educate or re-educate the consumers, and if we have the big guys making cheap stuff. Also, people who think wine should cost the same as a beer for instance just don't realize how much more time it takes to make wine (years longer!). As they say "time is money".

Did you find any aspect of setting up the company to be actually fun?

I really enjoyed building the website, brainstorming on creative ways to reach customers, writing newsletters and other marketing materials - and learning! You learn a lot when you set up a business!

What appeals to you about the business?

The wine business is challenging and many enthusiasts go into it thinking it is an easy career but those who own and operate a winery as a small business really are the old fashioned mom and pops type of Americans. We care about our reputation. We care about quality and relationships. Most of us also care about making wine, not necessarily making money.

What inspired the company name?

"Turiya" is a state of pure consciousness wherein reality and truth are harmonious. It basically means that you are absolutely aware. I liked this word because I believe that we should all be aware. Knowledge is power and en vino veritas! (In wine there is truth).

How did you come up with your logo and labels?

My label is elegant yet simple with a touch of femininity. It is the word "Turiya" screened on the bottles in 24k gold with a semi-equal to sign below the word (≈) That is to show that when you are in the state of Turiya reality is ≈ to truth. Back to the gold, wine is an item of luxury and so are the bottles! I do believe that if you take the time and energy to create a beautiful wine, the bottle should also be noteworthy. The label design is a reflection of that.

So you've got the business set up and then you have to figure out which products you will sell first. Some winemakers decide this before they even start their company. Which did you do?

It starts with an idea I suppose. I had the idea to make only wines I would personally drink, therefore I only make red wine (blends of red grapes as well as work with some of my personal favorite classic varietals). I created a business plan and outlined which varietals I would produce and which ones I wouldn't. The business was far from set up when I started making wine but I definitely knew what my lineup would look like - RED. I don't want to be mainstream so I try to work with varietals that are a bit more obscure and not often bottled alone. I also don't promise to make the same blend twice, nor do I promise that you can get a vertical of any varietal because I change it up so that I can stay small and produce several different varietals.

How do you go about developing your blends or vintages?

When I first started I thought I would use some of the standard California winemaking practices - especially when it came to the aging part, but as the wine got closer to the 20-22 month mark, where most wineries bottle, I tasted the wine from the barrel and it still seemed unfinished. I kept it in barrel another year and paid attention to the nose, the body, the finish. This third year of aging is where the layers of smells continued to build, the finish elongated, and the tannins continue to connect and form the silky texture I desired. Finally after three years the wine spoke to me saying "I'm ready!". I bottled it up and started tasting it all over again from the bottle to see how it was aging. By the time I felt the wine was ready for release it had been nearly 5 years. This has become my practice - to age the wines until I feel they are

ready and not release them until they have reached that point. I mean, I've already planned to wait for this glorious elixir, so why rush it at the end?

Where did you learn to develop a vintage?

I learned the most by doing (hands-on learning) and NOT doing (not manipulating by use of chemicals to [ironically] protect, enhance or remove flavors, color, texture, etc.). I'd never worked production for any other wineries but I had done my homework and was shocked at the things you can do to wine to enhance or 'fix' it. Before jumping in and doing it, I had already formed a plan for my first vintage - wine should be wine; pretty simply - fermented and aged grapes. Back then, I did a lot of freelance writing for various wine websites. I was fortunate enough to taste a lot of wines with an obligation to write about them, the winery, the people and sometimes money behind the wines, etc. In tasting others wines, interviewing those producers, finding out what they did to create each wine - in technical terms - was the start of my vintage development. I learned that I was a picky drinker! I learned what specific vineyards were best at growing my favorite varietals. I learned about the cost of production. I learned that there are a lot of small decisions in winemaking that make big differences. My small yet big decision in winemaking was to put the grapes through as little manipulation as possible. I wanted natural flavors so I went for some of the most well-farmed vineyards, harvested the fruit focusing on the grapes fruit and acid balance. It was important to me to make an ageable wine - I wanted ripe, but not overripe. After the harvest I watched over my babies and used all of my senses to make decisions. I let them soak up their own flavors for a few days before fermentation began. It tasted like the best juice on the face of the planet. I tested the basic chemistry of the grapes to make sure the fruit was healthy. I focused and adjusted my PH level to a safe number but tasted as I added it - sort of like adding salt to taste as you cook at home. After the fermentation the wine was barreled down and I pretty much crossed my fingers and figured, well, I did very little to disturb the creation of this wine, let's hope it is really that simple! As the wine developed naturally, I left it alone only to taste it here and there to see how the flavors were developing. I was also concurrently taking winemaking courses at Alan Hancock College.

What are some key ingredients and tools that you must have?

Grapes. You need grapes. You also need acid which can be found in the grapes but may sometimes need to be adjusted if the grape doesn't naturally have enough. Acids help by naturally protecting the wine from spoilage, it also helps to age wines longer, and gives wine the proper balance so that it excites your palate. If you are making more than a trash-can full, you probably want to use a de-stemmer, press, barrels and bottles, a forklift, a truck, various hoses, kegs...

Do you need someone to help you when you develop a vintage?

Yes and no. I don't own the big equipment like a crusher/destemmer or a press. I need other vintners who do own these items to allow me to process at their facility. I rely on the farmers to grow the fruit and manage the vineyards. Do I have employees? No. I process myself and sometimes have family members help with things like bottling, waxing bottles and the occasional punch-down - these things are all done entirely by hand. Have I ever used a consultant - no, not technically but when I began I was at a facility where there were several other vintners and being new to the process I went around asking these other vintners what their process was so that I could formulate my own plan. I also needed the education and science to prove to me that my plan would work, so you could also say that I needed the teachers.

What do you advise people to avoid when developing a wine label or vintage themselves?

I advise enthusiasts to do it as a hobby or work for another vintner before trying to jump into the business. I advise that they work for a winery (or several) to see how hard and how many hats each person wears and the logistics that go into the winery year round. I advise that if they are serious than they should really plan ahead and have a lot of money to throw at it. Lastly, I let them *know that there is not much money to be made in the industry and there is a lot of competition so be sure to be passionate about what you produce!*

So what do you want the buyer to come away with after tastings your creations?

Ah... so much! I want them to feel educated and aware of wine, not as a product but more so as an investment toward an experience. I want them to understand why wine is so special to me, how I have worked hard to craft each and every bottle of wine. I want them to get to know each grape and have a personal relationship with it. I want them to understand (by tasting) how those small winemaking decisions make big differences. I want them to feel inspired to live their own dream because I believe that anyone can reach their personal goals if they just focus on it! Anything is possible!

What are some of your favorite brands of wine?

I had the 2005 Alban Reva Syrah in a blind tasting and it blew my mind. Rudd 2006 Estate Cabernet was another unbeatable experience. Almost any Gevrey Chambertin...

Favorite winemaker?

Brett Escalera /Consilience and Tre Anelli. I was lucky to work for Brett from 2006-2011 and was fortunate to be in the inner circle of the company. I learned not only how hard you have to work during the harvest season but also throughout the rest of the year managing inventories, selling the wine and operating a tasting room. As the winemaker you are the face of the business; people would rather be talking to the winemaker than some salesperson. I got to hear some of his very eloquent yet passion infused reasoning behind each wine that he produced. I was fascinated that he could manage each harvest and eventually take on more and more. He also had several other wineries that he consulted for and amongst all that he would remember peoples names and was always so cordial.

Favorite food?

I might get in trouble for this from the animal lovers out there but I love Veal. When I was young my step-father (who is a chef) would make my favorite meal of Veal Schnitzel with a lemon butter caper sauce and a side of pasta - lightly buttered with some parmesan. Muah!

Favorite beer or spirit?

I am a gin gal. Ransom is my gin of choice on a whiskey day, or I veer towards Leopold's when I am in the mood for refreshing botanicals.

Favorite dessert?

Flourless chocolate lava cake.

Favorite movie with wine?

The first thing that pops into my mind is Scandal on ABC... not a movie but the main character is a rock-star chick and after her long, hard days, she starts and often finishes a bottle of high-end French something or the other. She makes it look so appealing I find myself going to my cellar and pulling out something to join her with.

Favorite book with wine?

Any book. If I have time to read, you bet I'm going to have a drink in hand.

What makes a winemaker different than or similar to other artisans such as chocolatiers, chefs, or fashion designers?

Good question. Other than the raw materials we work with, I don't believe we are very different.

When it comes to terroir and how it affects the wine, do you consider yourself a floral person, a musk person, a citrus person, a woodsy person, an earthy person, or something else?

Earthy. I even made shirts that say so.

Who is doing exciting things in the winemaking area, in your opinion?

I've become a big fan of Westerly Wines since Adam Henkel has taken over winemaking. I think Sashi Moorman has been doing great things in our area for years.

Are there any developments in the field that you find very exciting?

I tend to go for tradition over new technology. I don't think winemaking needs to be complicated. The less manipulation the better. I am excited for more vineyards to move toward organic, sustainable and biodynamic farming methods.

Has the internet helped?

Absolutely. I am very grassroots but use tools like Facebook, Twitter and Mailchimp to talk about wine.

Do you have advice for anyone wanting to get in the business?

Don't be afraid to ask questions (especially the question "WHY?"), ask for help, or admit to yourself that you don't know everything.

Do you have any advice on how they can make sure they have a profitable bottom line?

> Don't try to take over the world. Just make enough and price it accordingly so that the management aspect of the business doesn't become too much.

Do you think there are any benefits to private label wines for the winemaker?

> Yes, making private label stuff is good for everyone. It gives the consumer who wants to make wine, doesn't know how, and doesn't necessarily want to make a business of it, accessible. It gives the winemaker additional income.

What about tips for those who just want to drink and taste wine?

> Get out there and do it! I took extensive notes of the wines I tasted over the years and eventually started asking more questions and discovered correlations of the chemistry of wine to what I enjoyed drinking most. Travel if you can afford it and visit different wine regions. Try a local class on wine tasting and common varietals. My first book on wine was 'Wine for Dummies'. There are tons of great reference books out there so pick a few up! Watch YouTube videos and subscribe to RSS feeds for wine bloggers. There is a ton of information

out there and most of it is at your fingertips and free! Also, there are handy apps out there such as Vivino, Delctable and Cellartracker. These references can give you handy info on each wine, helpful for those drinkers who want to read reviews on the wines before buying or opening.

Joshua Ruiz

GENDER: Male

COMPANY NAME: Twisted Roots Winery

WEBSITE: Twistedrootsvineyard.com

YEAR COMPANY FORMALLY ESTABLISHED: 2009

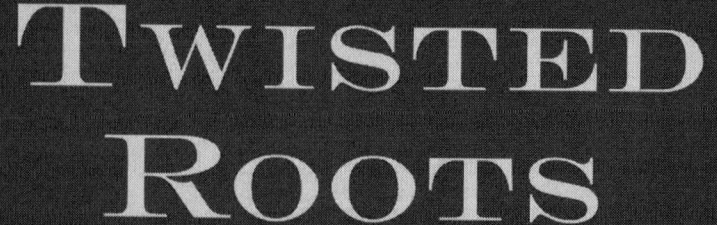

Apparently you love wine, what started the love affair?

While in college I had my first encounter with wine, given to me by my roommate. As I was not a fan of beer, like most of my friends at the time, I began to drink more and more wine. I soon became fascinated with finding out how the wine got its flavor.

How long have you been interested in wine?

Since the first drink in college

What's there anything from history, recent or ancient, that also drew you to the field?

NO, my interest is solely what I have experienced since college

What was the point of starting your own wine label?

After returning home from college, and marrying my wife, I got the opportunity to take my now passion for wine further. Her family, the Schmiedt family in Lodi, owned a vineyard that had been in the family or three generations. Ross Schmiedt, my wife's uncle, had been managing the family estate his entire life, and had crated the Twisted Roots label, with the idea of experimenting with winemaking. He got sick with ALS at the same time, and I saw this as an opportunity to carry on his project, as well do something for the family.

Is wine a luxury item?

Yes, I believe that wine is a luxury item, however I think it is also the great equalizer in modern times. I believe that while wine was once reserved for the wealthy or the high class, today wine has crossed over those lines, and become something that everyone can enjoy.

How did you go about starting the company from a small business standpoint?

Starting the company was the easiest part of the whole project. We simply put some funds into a bank account, filed some paperwork, and the "Company" was started.

What were some of the most important steps?

The most important step was making sure that we had all the proper paperwork filed with all of the proper authorities. We quickly found other winery owners who would help us thru the paperwork jungle, and I think that was the best/most important step of all. In the wine business, there are lots of people who want to help, you just have to ask.

Did you find any aspect of setting up the company to be actually fun?

I think the fun part of setting up the company was being able to work with family, and to spend time with Ross, who was sick. I look back now that Ross is gone, and I wish that I would have spent more time with him.

What appeals to you about the business?

For me the entire business comes down to the wine. I love the wine, I love the process of making the wine, and most of all I love the process of growing great grapes. Our philosophy is to let the grapes speak for themselves, which is why we spend so much time in the vineyard, versus the winery.

What inspired the company name?

We like to tell people that "if you knew our family... you would know how we came up with the name", however the true is not as fun. Ross, who was managing the family vineyard, one day pulled up

Twisted Roots

2008

Petite Sirah

LODI

one of our "1918" Old Vine Zinfandel vines, and the roots were twisted around each other, and he decided that would make a great name for a winery one day. He had the foresight to know that it was a good name, so before any wine was made he trademarked the name.

How did you come up with your logo and labels?

While designing the label and logo, Ross wanted something that would be unique, as well as something that would stand out on the shelf with all of the other wines. He also wanted something that was classic, clean, and had the appearance of success, which is how we came up with a label that goes across the bottle. Ross commented that when people win a competition, they are often presented with a sash, which when they put it on goes across their body. Everyone recognizes that as a winner. This is how the label come about: a sash.

So you've got the business set up and then you have to figure out which products you will sell first. Some winemakers decide this before they even start their company. Which did you do?

We decided before the company was officially organized which wine we would sell first, because the first year we had excess of our Petite Sirah, which the contracted winery did not want at harvest time. Now not only are we known for our Petite Sirah, but it has become my personal passion as the winemaker.

How do you go about developing your blends or vintages?

We do not make any blends at Twisted Roots, we are focused on making single varietal wines. As I mentioned before, we are farmers first, and spend our time focused on the vineyard. We believe in making wines that express all aspects of the varietal that we grow, and that means letting the grape speak for itself. Our job is to protect the grape in the vineyard, give it all the essentials that it needs to develop the great flavors that are unique to the varietal, and then get out of the way once it is in the winery. Simply put, we make all of our major decisions in the vineyard not the winery, we are farmers who make wine, not winemakers who farm.

Where did you learn to develop a vintage?

The great fun of making the wines and starting the company has been learning as we go. We have made each vintage of wine simply by our own tastes and preferences, with only a little advice from friends or family. We decided early on to make wine that we liked, and not worry about what other people thought, doing it our way.

What are some key ingredients and tools that you must have?

We believe that there is nothing you need to make wine other than your own tastes. Winemaking should not be about anything other than you trying to express yourself thru the wine, and therefore you don't need any special training, or knowledge, just a passion for it.

Do you need someone to help you when you develop a vintage?

Again I don't think that you need someone to tell you what you can and can't do, however you do need someone to help you work thru the winemaking process if you have never done it before.

What do you advice people to avoid when developing a wine label or vintage themselves?

I think that the one word of advice that I would tell people who want to make wine is make sure to express yourself, and develop a product that you love. There are lots of critics and people who want to tell you how it ought to be done, but I would suggest avoiding them in the beginning so that you can do your own thing.

So what do you want the buyer to come away with after tastings your creations?

Our goal for our customers is to walk away having enjoyed the wine we made, all the while we hope that they feel that they got more value out of the wine then they spent. We also want people to learn, and feel the underlying philosophy that the wine was made with; "We believe that good wine is best if shared with friends and family".

What are some of your favorite brands of wine?

If I had to choose another winery/wine that I really liked, other than ours, I would choose Tablas Creek in Paso Robles.

Favorite winemaker?

I don't know them, but the winemaker at Tablas Creek.

Favorite food?

I would say that my favorite food is pizza, it is easy, always good fresh, or the next day, and goes well with red wine.

Favorite beer or spirit?

I am not a beer guy at all, but I do like vodka.

Favorite dessert?

I am easy when it comes to desert, I like anything sweet.

What makes a winemaker different than or similar to other artisans such as chocolatiers, chefs, or fashion designers?

I think that winemakers are just the same as all of the different types of artists. We all make a product with passion, with our hands, and our hearts and souls. It doesn't really matter what the final product is, chocolate, wine, or something else, the end result is still the same....something great.

When it comes to terroir and how it affects the wine, do you consider yourself a floral person, a musk person, a citrus person, a woodsy person, an earthy person, or something else?

I think that terroir is real, and important, but again I think that for us we believe in the grape itself. What is wine if not a great expression of the flavors of the grape, and it done well, the terroir helps to showcase those.

Who is doing exciting things in the winemaking area, in your opinion?

I think it is hard to point to just one winery/person, as I believe the entire wine industry is doing new and great things all the time right now. I think that the age of following traditions is gone, and that everyone is free to express their own skills and thoughts.

Are there any developments in the field that you find very exciting?

I think that thing that is most exciting for me about the industry right now, is that wine is now so much more mainstream then ever before, and that all social/economic classes are buying wine, learning about wine, and enjoying wine.

Has the internet helped?

I am not sure how, but there is no doubt that the internet has helped grow and develop the wine industry into what it is today. I think that people of my generation have learned a lot on the internet, I even believe that there are winemakers that learned completely online, so yes it has helped.

Do you have advice for anyone wanting to get in the business?

My advice for someone who wants to get into the business is always the same... don't do it unless it is your passion, and it is in your heart. Like anything else, if you're not passionate about it, it will become much harder in the long run, and that always makes it difficult.

Do you have any advice on how they can make sure they have a profitable bottom line?

Profits are an ever moving target in this business, and what I would say is to start small, don't grow faster than your profits/income allow. Again if this is your passion, profits will not be as important.

Do you think there are any benefits to private label wines for the winemaker or the private labeler?

Yes, I think that given the number of labels on the market today, private label business is growing, and is going to continue to grow.

What about tips for those who just want to drink and taste wine?

If you just want to drink/taste wine, then do it, it's that simple. Don't worry about the so-called "Rules," or things that people say you have to do, or what you are supposed to like; find your own style. I have one rule, it is simple: Find what you like, and drink more of it. It makes no difference what the price point is, where the wine was made, it only matters that you like it.

Jon Affonso

GENDER: Male

COMPANY NAME: AH Wines

WEBSITE: AHWines.com

YEAR COMPANY FORMALLY ESTABLISHED: 2008-2009

Apparently you love wine, what started the love affair?

I began drinking wine as an exchange student in France. I graduated from Jesuit High School and I repeated my senior year at Lycée Francois Truffaut in Challans on the West Coast of France. I was given a fantastic education in French language and culture, which included wine.

How long have you been interested in wine?

I was 18 when I was an exchange student, and my consumption of wine continued when I returned to California. It continues to the present at 45 years of age.

Was there anything from history, recent or ancient, that also drew you to the field?

When I returned from France to California, my interest shifted to the wine regions of California. I had grown accustomed to drinking wine and the French wines I drank while in France were all but impossible to find in the US. I was born and raised in Sacramento and yet I had never been to Napa or Sonoma before. I quickly began exploring these regions, as well as wines from the Sierra Foothills. At this point I was strictly a consumer. I began college at CSU Sacramento and was working towards a degree in Geology. I was helping my Dad with his business as a coffee roaster. It was when I was about 2 years from graduating that I began looking at the job market and tried to figure out how my education would translate into a real job. I loved the study of geology as it blended the world of science with outdoor exploration and hiking. However, when I looked into the prospect of getting a job, the real world job did not appeal to me. So now I was in the middle of a career crisis. What was I going to do? It was then that I asked myself "What interests me that could be turned into a real job?" Wine was the perfect blend of my interests in science, French culture, and the satisfaction of creating a handcrafted product (like I did with coffee).

I began exploring the option of becoming a winemaker. I created a list of questions, and I called and interviewed several winemakers to determine if this was a career for me. I was hooked after the first call. Since I was too far along to give up my degree in Geology, I continued but with the idea of moving to a Master's degree in Enology. Upon completion of my Bachelor's Degree, I immediately moved and earned a Master's Degree in Enology from Fresno State.

What was the point of starting your own wine label?

AH Wines' main focus id to provide wines that are approachable, yet have layers of complexity that give the consumer a wine that is affordable and surpasses their expectations of quality with complexity and lusciousness. We believe that, like in France and many other parts of the world, wine is a beverage for all occasions and for everyone to enjoy. It enhances the health and well being of all and is an integral component in the culture of food.

Is wine a luxury item?

While wine can be a luxury item, the vast majority of times it is not. Wine in many parts of the world is very common and is as plentiful as any other beverage. Most of the time wine should be consumed and not collected. It brings more joy when it is shared than when it is stored.

What were some of the biggest challenges?

The biggest challenge in the wine industry is providing a wine that is of high quality and significantly different from other competing wines; and at a price point that is attractive to consumers. The problem with this formula is that wine is incredibly capital intensive and the rate of return can be very slow. With all of these elements, it makes it very difficult for anyone to be very profitable.

How did you come up with your logo and labels?

We have several wine labels that we produce wine under. In our opinion, a wine is a medium with which to connect to the consumer in such a manner as to persuade them to try our product the first time. It should not be used to promote one's self or one's family. Unfortunately, ego plays a heavy role in many wine labels. We conjure images that tap into a consumer's like and interests. Black Bear Red Chair plays to the childlike whimsy that is in all of us, while G. Washington taps into a patriotic yet elegant image that lets the consumer know this wine is more serious. These are but two extreme examples of our wine label's character. We have several in between.

How do you go about developing your blends or vintages?

We produce many different wines and there is a different development for each. The main idea for us is to recognize a trend in the marketplace and see how we might tap into that trend, and yet do something unique so as to differentiate ourselves. An example might be the increased interest in Cabernet Sauvignon of the millennial generation. Our goal would be to make a Cabernet that is not only true to its roots but gives something different for the younger generation to appreciate. This is accomplished by harvesting Cabernet Sauvignon from multiple regions and at different levels of development. We might have some more robust and tannic Cabernet from a coastal region and a lighter bodied more fruit driven Cabernet from further inland. These grapes are also picked at different developmental stages to lend further diversity and character. Each of these wines is fermented and barrel-aged in similar manners, using techniques that bring each wine's character to the surface. It is like a painter with his palette when it comes time to blend them. Then we will blend these wines so as to bring a balance of fruit and tannin that we believe will speak to our target audience. Once the blend is complete we then allow the wine about 6 months to further come together in the barrel. When the wines have integrated, they are ready to be cleaned up and prepared for bottling.

While we do produce many different wines, one thing remains the same; the desired characters must come from the fruit. We achieve these differences by harvesting different varieties, from different regions, and at different flavor progressions. This creates layers of complexity and interest in the wine. The complexity is then further involved with different yeast strains and barrel types and many other winemaking techniques. In the end, the more different lots you have to work with, the more layers of flavor and aroma will be developed to create a balanced wine.

Where did you learn to develop a vintage?

I learned to develop wine like any other profession; through education and experience. School taught me the theory behind fermentation, how to direct a fermentation in different directions with different techniques. Experience through trial and error has taught me that different levels of ripeness in different varieties lend different characteristics. In addition, different coopers, wood types, and toast levels in combination with different fruit characteristics provide a mixture of flavors and aromas that allow wine to be the most complicated and interesting matrix on the planet. It is these years of experience that have brought me to today.

What are some key ingredients and tools that you must have?

A wine must have structure from which to provide a foundation for other components. Structure is usually the tactile impression of the wine. "How does it feel in the mouth?" This might be the lighter weight of a crisp and refreshing white wine. It could also be the thick heavy weight of a late harvest Zinfandel. Achieving these goals is done by growing the selected fruits in certain areas and then harvesting them at different times when the fruit has the desired flavor profile. The most important winemaking decisions are basically A) where is the fruit coming from and B) when do you pick it.

Do you need someone to help you when you develop a vintage?

I need feedback from the sales staff and from consumers. These are my focus groups and the inspiration that I draw upon to create a wine. While I love to drink wine and I prefer to make wine that I love to drink, the reality is I will never be that thirsty. I can never drink it all. Therefore, I like and want to make wine that people enjoy. It is akin to having guests coming to your house for dinner. Do you want to make something you enjoy making or do you want to make something they will enjoy eating. It is great if you can do both, but that is not always possible. Given the choice I will always prefer to have happy guests.

What do you advice people to avoid when developing a wine label or vintage themselves?

The only advice I can give is to protect your wines from spoiling. Maintain clean and healthy winemaking practices so that the wines are allowed to develop into their own true selves. Beyond that, it is all subjective and winemakers should be allowed to experiment freely to develop any product they wish. Ultimately it is the market who is the final judge and not myself.

So what do you want the buyer to come away with after tastings your creations?

I want them to simply say "Wow, I would like another glass of that." It is all any winemaker can hope for.

What are some of your favorite brands of wine?

I know this is an indirect answer to a direct question, but there are too many brands to name and different brands sometimes specialize in different varieties. Unfortunately for this question, I like all varieties and styles in different situations. For example, I like drinking white wine in the summer and red wine in the winter. My taste changes with the seasons. I rarely gravitate to one brand but I enjoy experimenting and tasting as many as possible.

Favorite winemaker?

There are a few winemakers I truly admire. Scott Harvey and Paul Draper come to my mind. They have taken Zinfandel from a common status and elevated it to heights never dreamed of. Their serious approach to Zinfandel's growing and winemaking practices have shown the world that this variety has depth and diversity. The wines they have made and continue to make are considered to be the best that varietal has ever seen.

Favorite food?

French cuisine will always hold a special place for me. It brings me back to how this whole path started. French cuisine is like coming back to my second home.

Favorite beer or spirit?

As I get older I am gravitating away from beer and moving toward Whiskey (in the forms of Scotch, Irish Whiskey and Bourbon). I still like beer and I have recently moved from IPAs to more traditional German beer. I have found a love of Kolsch in a recent trip to Cologne.

Favorite dessert?

Again French Cuisine comes to mind. Profiteroles are my absolute favorite. These are a puff pastry stuffed with fresh whipped cream, or chocolate mousse, or even ice cream. These pastries are stacked and topped with either caramel, sugar glaze, or my favorite melted chocolate.

Favorite movie with wine?

I really enjoyed the documentary SOMM. It shows the world of "Cork Dorkness" in all of its glory. It shows the torment and the dedication it takes to become a Master Sommelier. It is a world that many outside of the wine industry do not even know exists and it is shocking the amount of culture, history, and effort that goes into simply learning almost everything there is to know about wine.

Favorite book with wine?

"Wine and War" is an excellent historical book that tells the story of five famous French families and their struggle to protect and save their product from falling into enemy hands. Each family is from a different wine region and from various points in history as well. It is an excellent example of the dedication of people in the wine industry.

What makes a winemaker different than or similar to other artisans such as chocolatiers, chefs, or fashion designers?

I think that there are more similarities than differences. They do create a tangible product that is consumed and appreciated by an interested public. They are called to use all of their creativity and toil non-stop for hours to create their own interpretation of the best version of what wine should be. They are often judged by a third party whose opinion is then heralded as the benchmark of their success or failure. Lastly, if successfully judged, their egos usually increase exponentially along with their celebrity status.

When it comes to terroir and how it affects the wine, do you consider yourself a floral person, a musk person, a citrus person, a woodsy person, an earthy person, or something else?

> I believe that Terroir encompasses not only the soil but also the climate, the training system, the trellis type, the rootstock, the canopy management, and the type of irrigation system. All of these factors have a special role in their influence on the quality of the fruit. As to which type I prefer, I love them all. Each has their own unique place in the world of wine. There is a place for all wine and it is simply a question of the time in which it is enjoyed.

Who is doing exciting things in the winemaking area, in your opinion?

> There are several winemakers doing exciting things. There is always experimentation going on to constantly improve or enhance characteristics in wine. Whether it is fermenting in concrete eggs or removing the crusher from your destemmer or recycling lees into red wines, there are always new trends and experiments that are exciting.

Are there any developments in the field that you find very exciting?

I love experimenting with various types of barrels. While this is not new, I have always and will always be fascinated by what the barrel environment does to wine. I say that barrels are magic. I love different oak types, cooper, toast levels, and grain sizes. They all contribute different flavors, aromas and lend even to the mouthfeel of a wine. I will always wonder, "What would that barrel do to this wine?"

Has the internet helped?

Like anything else, the Internet has allowed producers and consumers to be closer than ever. We can now often sell direct as consumer can contact producers direct for questions. It has revolutionized how we sell and market our product.

Do you have advice for anyone wanting to get in the business?

It is not for the faint of heart. It is very time consuming and often there is not as much profit as you would like. There is a mystique that wine is for the wealthy and therefore wineries must be very profitable. That is rarely the case. Wine is very expensive to produce and very slow to return the investment. People in this industry do it for the passion, not the money. There are much easier ways to make a buck.

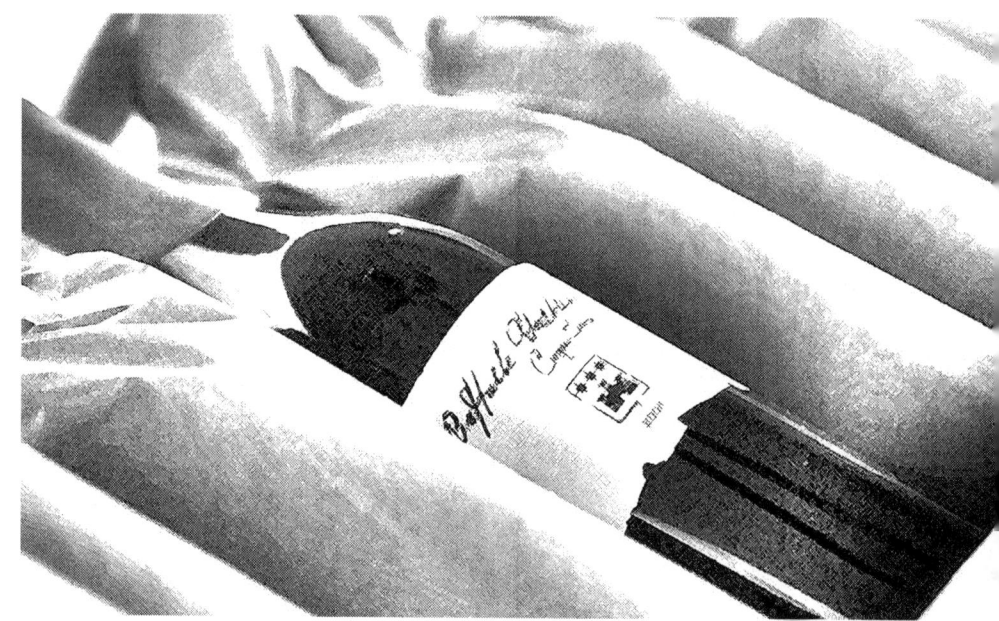

Do you have any advice on how they can make sure they have a profitable bottom line?

> Figure out what you want to make and what you can sell it for first. Then determine how much it will cost and what the expected profit should be. So often wineries simply produce the wine and say we will figure out how to sell it later. It should be the other way around. Many times wineries find themselves with a lot of wine that may not be in demand and they have to sell it for a loss.

Do you think there are any benefits to private label wines for the winemaker or private labeler?

> It depends on the winemaker who is making the private label. He or She may have an entirely different taste than you. It does not make theirs better, just different. It all depends on how the consumer values the wine.

What about tips for those who just want to drink and taste wine?

> My biggest tip for tasting wine is that your palette is unique to you and your preferences are just as valuable as anyone else's. Never be ashamed to say you like something just because it is not popular. Call it a guilty pleasure if you must but drink what you like and how you like it. It might make me cringe when my mother drinks my red wine with ice cubes, but she is entitled to enjoy her wine in any way she likes. There are no wrong answers and there are no wrong ways. Also try experimenting with food and wine pairings. It is fun and delicious.

Stacy Vogel

GENDER: Female

COMPANY NAME: Miner Family Winery

WEBSITE: minerwines.com

YEAR COMPANY FORMALLY ESTABLISHED: 1997

Apparently you love wine, what started the love affair?

My mother and I had a "Girls Night Out" shortly after I finished college. We went to a Wine Dinner featuring the wines of Shooting Star (now Steele Wines out of Lake County). The wine rep talked to us about how to taste wine, what characteristics and aromas you could find in wine, and I was fascinated. I ended up working for him a year later.

How long have you been interested in wine?

Since that dinner -- in 2000 I believe.

Was there anything from history, recent or ancient, that also drew you to the field?

I only started to learn some wine history once I started graduate school (at the University of California at Davis, for Viticulture and Enology). There is some fascinating history -- wine basically evolved and developed alongside humans in Europe over the last several thousand years.

What was the point of starting your own wine label?

I don't have one -- Miner wines are my "children" during the work week, and I go home to two human children outside of the office. I don't have room for any more!

Is wine a luxury item?

Wine can certainly be a luxury item, to be included in life's most special occasions. But there is a place for wine in our everyday life, as part of our daily meal, as part of unwinding at the end of the day, or as a part of sharing a moment or conversation with a partner or dear friend.

How do you go about developing your blends or vintages?

We have a series of blending sessions every spring to prepare the blends that will be bottled later in the summer. We taste each lot of wine that is fermented (for example, we may have 15 lots of Cabernet Sauvignon alone), and try several different potential blends of each wine. We may go through 50+ possibilities of our flagship wine, the Oracle, which contains 5 different grape varieties. We will alter oak levels, percentages of each variety, and levels of each of those 15 lots of Cabernet to find the best blend for that vintage. There are 6 of us who taste and rate all of these possible blends, and by consensus we decide which blend will make it into the bottle.

Where did you learn to develop a vintage?

I have been with Miner Family for over half of my career, so most of my winemaking skills have been developed here. I am lucky to have a great mentor in my boss, Gary Brookman.

What are some key ingredients and tools that you must have?

Yeast, Sulfur Dioxide, temperature control during fermentation, and a functioning nose!

Do you need someone to help you when you develop a vintage?

Making wine is a team effort. From the vineyard crew to the cellar crew to your blending team, no winemaker can do it alone.

So what do you want the buyer to come away with after tastings your creations?

I hope people can recognize the care that was taken to put our finished product into the bottle. Any given wine may or may not be your style, but everything we produce was made carefully and with intent. I hope that "truth" shines through.

What are some of your favorite brands of wine?

I am a big fan of both red and white Burgundy wines, white Sancerre, and great Champagnes. There are well-known producers that shine year after year -- Domaine Vacheron, Domaine de Montille, Louis Latour. Even the big guys like Mumm and Krug have fantastic wine. And traveling in those areas is such a joy, as you find amazing wines that never make it to our market.

Favorite winemaker?

So many people making wines of intent and passion that it would be hard to identify one in the entire world. Here in Napa, I find myself drawn to winemakers like Cathy Corison who chart their own path outside of current stylistic trends, and just keep getting better and better every year.

Favorite food?

Depends on the night. My husband wooed me with his Peking Duck and mushroom risotto. I almost never say no to sushi. Or a really good croissant.

Favorite beer or spirit?

Bourbon, on ice with a strong ginger beer and a squeeze of lemon.

Favorite dessert?

When a chocolate souffle is done perfectly, it is hard to beat.

Favorite movie with wine?

Any time my husband and I manage to sneak in a date night at the movies becomes my current favorite.

Favorite book with wine?

> The last book I read was called, "Your Three Year Old: Friend or Enemy?" That was read while drinking copious amounts of wine.

What makes a winemaker different than or similar to other artisans such as chocolatiers, chefs, or fashion designers?

> We only get to make wine once a year. It takes years to really understand a vineyard, a winery, and a variety. We don't get a do-over everyday. The pressure is on every time!

When it comes to terroir and how it affects the wine, do you consider yourself a floral person, a musk person, a citrus person, a woodsy person, an earthy person, or something else?

> There are lots of external things that can influence the wine. I've worked with a vineyard that has a big bay tree in the middle of it, and wine made from that section has a distinct bay leaf aroma to it. Pinot Noir in particular can be influenced by its surroundings, especially with woodsy characteristics.

Who is doing exciting things in the winemaking area, in your opinion?

> Anyone who has the extra fruit and space for a few little experiments each year can bring something exciting to the table. Nine Suns, a new winery on Pritchard Hill, a well-

known area for Cabernet Sauvignon, is growing a little bit of Grenache just to see how it does up there. Wrath, a winery in Monterey that is known for Chardonnay and Pinot Noir, planted a bit of Falanghina just to have fun with it.

Has the internet helped?

A bit: to research a new product or piece of equipment. But my network of colleagues and our collective experience is by far the most valuable thing when I have an issue with a wine or am pondering a new style or variety.

Do you have advice for anyone wanting to get in the business?

Only if you love it! Join us!

What about tips for those who just want to drink and taste wine?

Try new things! Seek advice from your wine shop clerk or the wine buyer at the restaurant. Try a variety you've never had before. There is so much wine out there to be discovered!

Doug Beckett

GENDER: Male

COMPANY NAME: Peachy Canyon Winery

WEBSITE: Peachycanyon.com

YEAR COMPANY FORMALLY ESTABLISHED: 1988

Apparently you love wine, what started the love affair?

My love affair started in 1981 when I moved my family from San Diego to Paso Robles to raise my boys in the country. My wife and I had been teaching in SD for about 9 years before moving. Our sons were 6 and 8 and we felt we wanted a different experience so the move. We bought a 20 acre walnut ranch with a beautiful old home about 6 miles west of Paso Robles on Peachy Canyon Road. It was in 1982 that I was introduced to Pat Wheeler who owned a small winery producing 100 cases called Tobias Winery. After working with Pat on a bottling we decided to become partners and the rest is history. We stayed together until 1987, dissolved the partnership and in 1988 Nancy and I started Peachy Canyon with the help of our boys and no partners. We kept our day jobs for many years and today we produce 50,000+ cases of premium wines that are sold throughout the US and many foreign countries.

How long have you been interested in wine?

For over 40 years. Actually my first interest was in high school, when I got together with a friend and we took enough grapes from his parents' back yard to start a 5 gallon batch of wine. The wine was terrible but we drank it, got a buzz, and got sick as well. My present interest started when I was a young teacher and a group of us started a wine group to explore different wines from different countries.

What was the point of starting your own wine label?

Once I fell in love with the idea of making wine there was no turning back. The love affair began in earnest when we started Peachy. It became a challenge, and I guess I did not want to just walk away because Tobias did not work. I also did not want anyone to be able to say, "I told you so, Doug was never a winemaker." I guess we fooled them.

Is wine a luxury item?

No, wine is for everyone and everyone should be able to find a wine they like. It also makes a great meal even better.

How did you go about starting the company from a small business standpoint?

I started in 1988 with barrels loaned to me by Chris Johnson, the winemaker for Hoffman Mountain plus a couple of tons of grapes fronted by famous Zinfandel grower, Bennie Dusi. Bennie said pay me when you can, and within several months he was paid off. I returned the barrels after a couple of years. It was in 1991 that Peachy Zinfandel was recognized as one of the Top 100 Wines in the World and the doors opened. Distributors wanted our wine and banks wanted to lend us money. Oh, how the times have changed.

What were some of the most important steps?

Learning how to make exceptional wine and selling it.

What were some of the biggest challenges?

I have always said, the winery has to be a business first and a love affair second. That says so much, without the financing we would not be here, and had we not been able to sell our wine we would not be here. We still work with the bank but have been able to keep it family-owned with no outside investors or partners.

Did you find any aspect of setting up the company to be actually fun?

It's all fun, just a little more challenging than many other businesses. Wineries and Restaurants are the two most challenging businesses I know of, and two of the businesses many people fantasize on owning. Both are great ways to go broke.

What appeals to you about the business?

It's the only business I know of where you often get "atta boys and girls" for something you love. Most jobs don't offer that kind of positive feedback on a regular basis (unless you make crappy wine). I really enjoy being behind the table sharing my art form.

What inspired the company name?

I lived in Peachy Canyon on Peachy Canyon Road. The canyon and road were named for an old horse thief named Peachy who would hide stolen stock in caves out in the canyon. Old Peachy wound up on the wrong end of a rope.

How did you come up with your logo and labels?

My old house is on the label.

So you've got the business set up and then you have to figure out which products you will sell first. Some winemakers decide this before they even start their company. Which did you do?

I love Zinfandel so it was natural that I start with something I love. It also gave me the chance to brand myself as a zin guy. I now make a total of 24 wines, way too many, of which 9 are zinfandel

How do you go about developing your blends or vintages?

Some of our blends are field blends which is the way zin was planted 100 years ago. Pick the varietals that work together, plant together, and you have a blend. We spend the life of the wine

in barrels tasting and doing experimental blends with other wines that we have in stock. Being at 50,000 cases, we have a very large spice rack to choose from. Like cooking, the more you have to work with the more creative you can be. We make wines to our taste that we think we can sell. We are like any successful artist, be they dancers, trumpet players, chiefs or actors. We strive to set ourselves apart from other winemakers, do what we love and hope we can sell it.

So what do you want the buyer to come away with after tastings your creations?

I want them to take some home and tell their friends. Join my wine club and let's stay friends for life.

What are some of your favorite brands of wine?

Biale, Saddleback Cellars, Tables Creek, Three Wine Co., Saduri, Chronic Cellars

Favorite winemaker?

The winemakers that made a difference for Peachy Canyon in the last 30 years: Toby Schumrick, Tom Westberg, Robert Nadeau, Josh Beckett and Rob Henson.

Favorite food?

Black Truffle Risotto

Favorite beer or spirit?

Crafted IPA's

Favorite dessert ?

Anything chocolate

What makes a winemaker different than or similar to other artisans such as chocolatiers, chefs, or fashion designers?

The only thing that makes us different is some of us can sell our product and make a living, and most cannot. My favorite example, some folks can get $50 for their scrambled eggs and many can't give theirs away.

When it comes to terroir and how it affects the wine, do you consider yourself a floral person, a musk person, a citrus person, a woodsy person, an earthy person, or something else ?

I believe I am more of a fruit forward person. I don't like to mask alcohol with oak or a lot of sugar. I want my wines to be veritably correct and exceptional. Why hide what Mother Earth gave us.

Who is doing exciting things in the winemaking area, in your opinion?

In Paso Robles we have several stand outs that have made a difference, such as Justin Smith, Matt Trevisan, and Bob Hass.

Has the internet helped?

Tremendously, e-commerce has expanded as has our exposure internationally

Do you have advice for anyone wanting to get in the business?

It's easy to get into, however there are only two things I stress when folks are wanting to get into the business:

1 - You have to sell your wine
2 - You have to sell your wine.

Do you have any advice on how they can make sure they have a profitable bottom line?

Understand the cost of making wine and doing business. Without these tools you will never be profitable

Do you think there are any benefits to private label wines for the winemaker?

No, for this to be profitable you have to have volume or you go broke. The more volume, the greater the investment, the more to lose.

What about tips for those who just want to drink and taste wine?

First taste as many wines as you can, go to tastings and visit tasting rooms. Drink water between tasting rooms and spit. If you go to a table or tasting room and don't care for the first two wines then leave. The chances of you finding one if you continue are slim and none. When you find a wine you like, buy it. You will be able to share your experience and pair it with something you like. Always remember, the wine taste better when you are with the winemaker or owner, or drinking too much. Just buy the wines you like.

Anthony M Truchard II

GENDER: Male

COMPANY NAME: Truchard Vineyards

WEBSITE: Truchardvineyards.com

YEAR COMPANY FORMALLY ESTABLISHED: 1974

Apparently you love wine, what started the love affair?

I really had no choice in the matter. My brother and I have been working in the vineyards for as long as I can remember. In high school I began working in the cellar, so my first introduction to wine came before I could even legally drink it. I guess I first really started to appreciate the art of wine when I graduated from high school. Unlike many of my classmates, who went to sunny warm beaches to celebrate the last summer before college, I headed to Bordeaux to visit our previous intern and toured some of the wine regions of southern France. It was there that I learned wine is a part of everyday life.

How long have you been interested in wine?

I really began at an early age, so I feel I can say the majority of my life. I didn't always drink, but at the age of eleven I knew there was a difference between Chardonnay and Cabernet.

Was there anything from history, recent or ancient, that also drew you to the field?

I was a Philosophy and Biology major as well as studying art in college. I think that there is always a great overlap between these disciplines and wine. I love the Ancients' comparison of wine and euphoria.

What was the point of starting your own wine label?

> In 1989, after selling grapes for fifteen years and everyone telling us what a great reputation our grapes had, we decided to use some of our own grapes and make wine. The result, as you can see from the 25+ years of making wine, has been wonderful. Our wines have been at dinner tables all over the country, including The White House, and it is truly a pleasure sharing the joy of wine with so many people throughout the country and the world.

Is wine a luxury item?

> Not in our family. Every meal at home is enjoyed with wine. Yes, we have special bottles for special occasions, but at mealtime there is always a bottle of wine on the table.

What were some of the biggest challenges?

> Our biggest challenge is Mother Nature. You never know what she is planning.

Did you find any aspect of setting up the company to be actually fun?

Hiring people; finding personalities and passions that work well together and elevate everything we do.

What appeals to you about the business?

My favorite aspect of the wine industry is the vertical integration. We do everything to plant the vines, grow the grapes, harvest, make and sell the wine. We are involved in every aspect of the wine and grape business.

I also love sharing this passion and hard work with others when they open a bottle of our wine.

What inspired the company name?

It is our family name. The original Truchards came from France in the late 1880's to start a winery outside of Houston, Texas. Unfortunately not a success, but they did pass along a grape-growing tradition.

How did you come up with your logo and labels?

Our "Gold Barn" logo comes from the original Truchard winery that my great grandfather built in the 1880's in Texas.

Our label is a landscape of the hills that encompass our vineyards. Chuck House, the artist who designed the label, used the soils of our property as the color template. The shades of brown, gray and black show the diversity of our soils. We also have fog rolling over the hills to show the cool fog that keeps Carneros cool.

So you've got the business set up and then you have to figure out which products you will sell first. Some winemakers decide this before they even start their company. Which did you do?

We had the advantage of selling grapes for about 20 years before we started making wine. We gained a lot of experience from working with the grapes on our property and knew that Chardonnay, Pinot Noir,

Merlot and Cabernet Sauvignon were well suited for our property and our market.

How do you go about developing your blends or vintages?

We are a family business and make the decision as a family, along with our winemaker Sal Delanni. We blind taste through each wine and various blends, each of us deciding independently which ones we like. Then we make a case for why this should be the wine that we bottle. After making that decision, the winemaker unveils the blends. Our focus is always to express the grape and the Carneros region. We are farmers first and try not to interfere too much with the grape's natural flavors.

Where did you learn to develop a vintage?

Working in the cellar under our previous winemakers, Michael Havens and Ken Bernards. Both went on to continue their own labels, but we still use some of the traditions that they brought to the winemaking aspects of Truchard.

What are some key ingredients and tools that you must have?

Grapes and tanks. We keep winemaking pretty simple.

Do you need someone to help you when you develop a vintage?

> Our winemaker, Sal Delanni, is really the maestro behind the wines. He has been at the winemaking helm for the past 18 years. We do not believe in consulting winemakers. We want to make wines that express the personality and individuality of our site and farming.

What do you advise people to avoid when developing a wine label or vintage themselves?

> We tell them that it is a full time job and that you have to devote all your time and passion to it. It looks a lot easier from the outside, but the rewards are great.

So what do you want the buyer to come away with after tastings your creations?

> I want them enjoy the wines and to appreciate the artistry and individuality of the wine.

What are some of your favorite brands of wine?

> I enjoy wines from around the world, but what I enjoy drinking most are my friends' wines. I know how hard they have worked and how passionate they are about the wines they have made. To me a good wine is like a story and the more you know about the wine, the person, and what they went through to make the wine, the greater the appreciation.

Favorite winemaker?

> One that doesn't make the wine, but allows the grape to express itself.

Favorite food?

> Vietnamese food.

Favorite beer or spirit?

> On a hot day, a great margarita or mojito. On a cold night, a dram of Scotch.

Favorite dessert?

> Not much of a dessert person, I would prefer a glass of Madeira.

Favorite movie with wine?

"It's a Wonderful Life" with Champagne (This is a tradition that my wife and I have every Christmas)

Favorite book with wine?

Anything by Hemingway, his short terse sentences are easy to read even after a few glasses.

What makes a winemaker different than or similar to other artisans such as chocolatiers, chefs, or fashion designers?

I think a great winemaker is so much a creator, but also someone who observers and steers the wine if it goes astray. Left to their own, grapes will make themselves into wine. It is the winemaker's job to make sure that it doesn't go off course (i.e.. gets oxidized). My belief is the less influence the winemaker tries to exert on the wine the better. Of course this comes from someone who is focused on the vineyards.

When it comes to terroir and how it affects the wine, do you consider yourself a floral person, a musk person, a citrus person, a woodsy person, an earthy person, or something else ?

I would say a woodsy earthy person with a hint of Floral. One of my favorite grapes is Nebbiolo, which can exhibit all of these.

Who is doing exciting things in the winemaking area, in your opinion?

I think there is exciting wine being made from all parts of the world right now. People are really experimenting and finding what works for their location and their palates.

Are there any developments in the field that you find very exciting?

Yes, I think the movement away from critic's scores is a good thing. I think that the critics had their role and importance in removing a lot of bad wine from the market, but when wine making shifted to pleasing critics as the primary goal, many wines lost their individuality or soul. I like wine with a bit of personality. I think the digital age where everyone is a critic is good for wines. Several styles of wine can emerge from this, rather than everyone trying to please one or two people.

Do you have advice for anyone wanting to get in the business?

Yes, do it for the lifestyle and for the passion, but it is not easy work.

Do you have any advice on how they can make sure they have a profitable bottom line?

Make sure that you start with good capital, there are a lot of expenses upfront and you likely will not have anything to sell until after two or three years after you begin. This is how long it takes to make and age the wine.

What about tips for those who just want to drink and taste wine?

The most important thing is drinking what you like and continuing to try new things. Don't listen to experts telling you what to drink and like, drink the wines you think are delicious.

Dan Goldfield

Gender: Male

Company Name: Dutton-Goldfield Winery

Website: Duttongoldfield.com

Year Company Formally Established: 1999

Apparently you love wine, what started the love affair?

> I started drinking wines in my teens with my older brother (along with all the other things he turned me on to). Burgundies were his love, so they were my first. A 1969 DRC Richebourg was my first real epiphany, in 1976. I've always been an outdoors guy, and loved to travel – I was totally captivated by the combination of topography (I'd lay in bed and study the topo maps in Hugh Johnson's Word Atlas of Wine), culture, craft and hedonism – still am.

How long have you been interested in wine?

> 40 years

What's there anything from history, recent or ancient, that also drew you to the field?

> Not particularly, other than the intertwining of wine and history – how cultures always brought grape vines to wherever they expanded, from the Romans to Burgundy, to the Italians to California.

What was the point of starting your own wine label?

> Independence, both creatively and personally. I worked for a larger company, running two of their rapidly growing brands – great people, great brands – but I didn't want to choose between being a craftsman or executive, so needed to start my own.

Is wine a luxury item?

> Totally not – it's great food essentially. The move toward luxury marketing for economic reasons is a sad current reality and hard to resist if one wants to make the quality of wines I love. The sad thing is that so many who should be drinking these wines don't get to. I was drinking the most revered Burgundies when I was broke, but can't afford them now – just a sad reflection of our current world. It's modern America.

How did you go about starting the company from a small business standpoint?

My partner and I each put in some cash, rented custom crush space, and bought enough fruit for about 2,000 cases of wine. We worked on our wines at the end of our real job days – then I quit my full time job, started some consulting, and worked mostly on our project.

What were some of the most important steps?

First bank line of credit, finding the highest quality fruit we could, finding the time to do it right.

What were some of the biggest challenges?

Setting up a distributer network, wading through the regulatory maze (not a natural instinct for the winemaker type).

Did you find any aspect of setting up the company to be actually fun?

Totally! The excitement of crafting our new business was wonderful, the camaraderie of working with my partner, crafting wine that was purely for us was both fun and a touch scary. In general, folks in our business were tremendously supportive and helpful in giving ideas and sharing their experiences – I totally enjoyed talking with respected peers who had been there happy to help me.

What appeals to you about the business?

The people – lots of interesting folks who have made real choices for their own lives. The craft of winemaking. The interplay between natural cycles beyond our control, and creative thinking to respond. The continuously varying demands throughout the year, as opposed to repetitive tasks. The beautiful place I get to live, and the camaraderie with other people involved in agriculture, not just in the grape business.

What inspired the company name?

Just our names.

How did you come up with your logo and labels?

The wife of a winemaker friend is a graphic designer, and she gave us options to choose from.

So you've got the business set up and then you have to figure out which products you will sell first. Some winemakers decide this before they even start their company. Which did you do?

Being a winemaker, I did the former – probably not the best choice. The more advance marketing planning the better in this day and age.

How do you go about developing your blends or vintages?

I make wine from vineyards I love, and hone over the years. My blends are made systematically and blind in conjunction with my assistant winemaker. Our company style is to make the wines we personally love, from the inside out. We use fruit from many different vineyards - the best rise to the top and become designates, but never the first year - we like to get to know a vineyard before featuring it. Each wine we make goes through series of tastings with small variations to choose the final products.

Where did you learn to develop a vintage?

My master's degree is in enology from Davis, but I learned wine though experience working for other people, paying attention and collecting data from my own experiences, and listening carefully to the experiences of others.

What are some key ingredients and tools that you must have?

Attention to detail and stamina are probably the most important attributes; honesty about wines you made that just aren't so good (and therefore should not be included in your blend). Colleagues and coworkers to bounce ideas and wines in progress off of are key. Thoughtful analytical work and data usage are important to me, both for ultimate gustatory quality and quality control for consistency to our customers.

Do you need someone to help you when you develop a vintage?

> Don't know about need, but it's certainly always best in my case to have 2nd and third opinions.

What do you advise people to avoid when developing a wine label or vintage themselves?

> Insular thinking, cellar palate, ever putting something you don't love in a bottle with your name on it.

So what do you want the buyer to come away with after tastings your creations?

> That this product was well crafted, and reflected the place of its origin.

What are some of your favorite brands of wine?

> Williams Selyem, Compte De Vogue, Mascarello, Marquis De La Guiche, Shafer, Sauzet, Schlos Gobelsberger.

Favorite winemaker?

> Hard question – lots of good ones. Jeff Mangahas at Williams Selyem is a great craftsman.

Favorite food?

> Lots – fresh local Sonoma vegetables, fresh salmon, local fresh bread, sushi.

Favorite beer or spirit?

> Craft Bourbons and Ryes, fresh pale ales.

Favorite dessert ?

> Homemade ice cream.

Favorite movie with wine?

> "Muscle Shoals" – great music and great wine – perfect.

Favorite book with wine?

> "The Emerald Mile" – great true story of adventure, human spirit, environmental reality and wild nature. Awesome late night reading with a glass of anything.

What makes a winemaker different than or similar to other artisans such as chocolatiers, chefs, or fashion designers?

Very similar in many ways. We take a natural product and try to craft it to a personal vision. Like all crafts, we have many tools at our disposal, and the better we know the details of our tools, and particularly their limitations, the better we ply our craft. The best craftsperson knows when to do nothing. The biggest difference is that if something goes wrong it's another whole year before we get to try again. The continuous variation of our raw material is probably highest in winemaking. I frequently compare us with woodworkers.

When it comes to terroir and how it affects the wine, do you consider yourself a floral person, a musk person, a citrus person, a woodsy person, an earthy person, or something else ?

> Terroir is a complicated concept – it includes, land, people, facility, flora...I think of our neighborhood as offering vivid fruit, freshness, focus and precision.

Who is doing exciting things in the winemaking area, in your opinion?

> There are lots of new tools and concepts, but attention to basics and our land is the most important thing. For me, this question is covered in my favorite wineries.

Are there any developments in the field that you find very exciting?

> The most exciting developments locally come from people getting to know their land better and better, and matching plant material and farming to the place. Farming that is sustainable and respectful of the long term in every way (environmental impact, social awareness, fruit quality) is a great current focus.

Has the internet helped?

> For communication, yes;
> for focus and creativity, often no.

Do you have advice for anyone wanting to get in the business?

> Do what you love – work incredibly hard – don't give up if you care.

Do you have any advice on how they can make sure they have a profitable bottom line?

> Less is better than more – excess inventory is death.

Do you think there are any benefits to private label wines for the winemaker or the private labeler?

> They can be a great use for excess inventory, and good for trade relations. The best wine should always be the ones with your name on it.

What about tips for those who just want to drink and taste wine?

> Learn what you like – don't' worry about trends and pretense. It's all for fun – enjoy!

Damian Grindley

GENDER: Male

COMPANY NAME: Brecon Estate

WEBSITE: Breconestate.com

YEAR COMPANY FORMALLY ESTABLISHED: 2012

Apparently you love wine, what started the love affair?

My original passion was growing things and having an intimate understanding of plant physiology, culminating in a horticultural science degree. The wine trade is something that drifted into my life. It started with a part time job at a wine retailer/wholesaler in the UK that had a tasting counter. I worked my way from an assistant manager position through branch manager. Next step was taking all the precursors for the masters of wine. One day I looked at my hands, realized I wanted to be a little more hands on, and decided to do a masters of winemaking program in Australia. I never looked back.

How long have you been interested in wine?

My first exposure to wine was my father making kit wines when I was a teenager. Suspect this may have planted the original seed.

What's there anything from history, recent or ancient, that also drew you to the field?

No, however my other passions are cave exploration and science. The two are strangely interrelated, as many iconic wine regions are underlain by limestone. A winemaking career has also enabled me to be immersed in cave country, discover and map many tens of miles of passages formed millennia ago, and develop a keen interest in the relationship between flavor and calcareous soils.

What was the point of starting your own wine label?

After working in the wine trade for decades, I always said that I would never be crazy enough to start my own label. I've watched too many underfunded brands without a real home or soul come and go. Ironically, I was launching successful brands for other people on a regular basis. So waiting all these years enabled me to learn what not to do. The once in a lifetime opportunity came along to start a winery and now here I am three years into this project wishing I had started it much earlier in life.

Is wine a luxury item?

I suspect this depends on your perspective. I would say for most of the planet's population it is a luxury item. However for some cultures or segments of society, wine is as much a staple as a cold beer at the end of a hard day.

How did you go about starting the company from a small business standpoint?

The industry segment we were looking at is fairly capital intensive, hence the need for a financial partner to help with seed money. In fact our reputation for launching successful brands was such that investors were seeking us out.

What were some of the most important steps ?

Funding.

What were some of the biggest challenges?

With all of the paperwork and hoop jumping, getting a winery license is extremely difficult, especially when you and your financial partners are not US citizens. The same applies to opening a bank account post-9 1 1. The onus is on you to prove it's not terrorist/drug money! We even had the right people on board to help us and the property already had an existing winery. There seems to be no incentive to change the process as companies who already have the licenses want to keep it as difficult as possible so it is a disincentive for others wanting to join the industry, which is a shame.

Did you find any aspect of setting up the company to be actually fun?

The process is a great learning curve and certainly pushes you into areas that you would never normally get pushed into. However, when you're in the thick of it, fun is not a word that spring to mind. Finally getting the property in hand and formulating a plan for the renovations with the architects was where the endless tide of paperwork started to morph into something more appealing.

What appeals to you about the business?

Having been in the industry in one form or other for almost three decades I now really do think it's a lifestyle choice. Great food and wine usually in a charming semi-rural area which is a safe place to bring up a family.

What inspired the company name?

The name Brecon Estate was inspired by our Welsh heritage and the enigmatic windswept Brecon Beacons National Park in South Wales. The Brecon Beacons are underlaid by Limestone which ties in with the Calcareous soil component that is a large part of our Vineyards terroir. We are also cavers who map and explore caves throughout the world. Our Winemaker explored and mapped many of the caves in the Brecon Park. The connections with our name are very personal and have a lot of meaning to us, but overall it is a short, strong name that was not trademarked in the US and has no other connotations in the USA.

How did you come up with your logo and labels?

We were renovating our winery from this bizarre cross between a rundown Spanish mission and an industrial sized Taco Bell, complete with neon, to something much more modern with clean lines and lots of comfortable earth tones and natural materials. We wanted the label to tie into what ironically became an award winning piece of architecture so that overall the Brecon Brand was cohesive. Lots of clean lines; a modern version of understated elegance. Of course you bring in a label designer to help achieve these noble goals. We have been very happy with the result.

So you've got the business set up and then you have to figure out which products you will sell first. Some winemakers decide this before they even start their company. Which did you do?

If your brand is like Brecon, which is all about a sense of place and the local terroir, then that automatically frames your choices. Our goal was to produce world class varietals from

our particular neck of the woods, so we are not tied to one particular old world genre or another. You will see Cabernet Franc and Malbec side by side with Syrah and Mourvèdre. Paso Robles is also understandably all about blends, as the diverse micro climates enable a wide range of varietals to reach world class status. It's a fun aspect of winemaking and really ties in with our cave exploration mentality. The other driver when purchasing the property was the 23 acres of old vine plantings of Cabernet Franc and Cabernet Sauvignon. Wonderful fruit, fantastic wine, so of course you are going to lead with these Estate offerings. The wine club dynamic also frames your choices. You need to offer variety and interest to sustain the club. Offering ten different versions of the same varietal from a single vineyard is unlikely to do that.

How do you go about developing your blends or vintages?

Vintage planning is constantly changing and starts years before an actual vintage is planted. You must have a style in mind and understand the varietal mix, clones, vineyards, barrels and winemaking techniques that will get you there. As the vintage approaches fruition, the barrel choices may change and evolve depending on how previous vintages have worked out. The weather during harvest and the various fruit yields will also have an impact. Consequently, what in your minds eye might have been a great vintage plan that even looked good on paper, by the time you come to the actual blending a couple of years later, may have radically changed. Sales in the interim often have an impact as one particular product may take off. So I guess the trick is to remain flexible. Sure co-ferment or blend some components early for better integration, however don't completely back yourself into a corner so that you can't tweak or steer the blend in a slightly different direction at the last minute.

Where did you learn to develop a vintage?

I first started in larger companies by putting together a final blend and then vintage planning. Seeing those thousands of vineyard lots passing through really does give you the ability to identify regionality and exceptional vineyards within those regions. In reality, this experience is a little like dog years for you may come across a particular situation once every few vintages in a smaller winery. Yet in a larger winery you might see it ten times with each vintage and consequently better understand how to handle it. However, it is not until working in the smaller wineries that the whole blending thing compared with the age-ability of a wine really gelled together.

What are some key ingredients and tools that you must have?

When you have no recipe but rather adapt to the fruit nuances that come into the winery in different years, it's actually the kit bag containing the range of things you can use that becomes the most important. Winemakers generally have a great array of options these days.

Do you need someone to help you when you develop a vintage?

Not so much these days. I will bounce some blends off some non winemaker wine consumers, or the tasting room staff — after all they are the ones who have to sell the wine and giving them ownership in a blend can be quite important. They tend also to be quite perceptive.

What do you advise people to avoid when developing a wine label or vintage themselves?

Remember if you wait until the wine is perfect before you bottle it, it will be on the downhill by the time it reaches the consumer. Make sure a label pops in a lineup in a liquor store if that's your market. Labels for example with too much fillary just don't stand out.

So what do you want the buyer to come away with after tastings your creations?

A sense of place. Varietals that show through, every wine is different but good and there is not an overly heavy stamp of oak or an overbearing house style.

What are some of your favorite brands of wine?

Cloudy Bay. Five Minutes by Tractor, 5th and Maple, Sea Smoke. Evocative names.

Favorite winemaker?

My favorite winemakers are the ones that have done the hard yards. Any fool given enough money, great barrels, and wonderful fruit can make one awesome wine. The trick is to make every wine in your portfolio an award winner. Having a family winery handed to you on a plate with existing wine styles and fantastic fruit does not necessarily make a well rounded dedicated winemaker. Consequently, I listen carefully to passionate winemakers with unusual backgrounds who have quit everything and traveled the world for wine. They have the knowledge to find wonderful fruit and create exciting wine styles which don't necessarily conform to regional norms.

Favorite food?

I'm not quite your typical winemaker. I prefer to drink tea, not coffee. I'm also not a great fan of cheese and I detest olives. However I love a damn good Indian curry or a Cornish pasty. I suspect it's my British upbringing and to be honest, not every bottle of wine is drunk with a fancy cheese plate.

Favorite beer or spirit?

I was a lover of beer for a long time and am now enjoying exploring the hard cider craft, especially the individual varietal ones as they really cleanse the palate. Spirit wise it has to be a peaty Islay malt. Not necessarily to drink but certainly to saver the aromas for hours at a time.

Favorite dessert ?

Pavlova

Favorite movie with wine?

"Love Actually" with a NZ Sauvignon Blanc

Favorite book with wine?

Life is too short to read a book twice. I'm a big fan of Sci-fi because it lets the mind wander beyond the day to day and think big picture possibilities. The accompanying wine is seasonal. If I am sitting curled up in front of the log fire contemplating some far flung galaxy then a liquor muscat or a meaty Syrah may be the tipple of choice. Whereas a balmy summer day relaxing on the porch with a zesty Albarino may be the preferred refreshment.

What makes a winemaker different than or similar to other artisans such as chocolatiers, chefs, or fashion designers?

Time, which is the fourth dimension, is the simple answer. Other artisans are creating the perfect piece to be enjoyed at that moment (ie Chef), or an unchanging piece that might be the pinnacle of perfection like a sculpture. Whereas wine is constantly changing as tannins coalesce and oxygen incorporates. In the end, the wine needs to be approachable in its early years in bottle, where it changes relatively rapidly. Then it goes through some adolescent phases before finally becoming something quite wonderful in adulthood.

When it comes to terroir and how it affects the wine, do you consider yourself a floral person, a musk person, a citrus person, a woodsy person, an earthy person, or something else?

None of the descriptors in the question are really driven by terroir, which for us is reflected in the acid balance and ripeness of the fruit or sometimes its minerality.

Who is doing exciting things in the winemaking area, in your opinion?

The South Africans seem the most innovative in research/new commercial wine styles at the moment. Interesting people generally make interesting wines.

Are there any developments in the field that you find very exciting?

It's a field that's been around for 3000 years so it's not quite like the tech industry for new developments. However in some overseas labs they seem to be taking baby steps with GMO yeast. While we want to be GMO free in our industry intellectually the results could be interesting or rather problematic.

Has the internet helped?

Absolutely. In every aspect of the business from winemaking to sales and marketing. We would not have the wine club or the social media reach without it

Do you have advice for anyone wanting to get in the business?

The great thing about the wine industry is there are so many ways to skin it. Know your plan and market segment. If small and boutique is your direction then it's location, location, location all the way. Be prepared to think out of the box. Golden Gate Park may be a better location than a hard to find country lane.

Do you have any advise on how they can make sure they have a profitable bottom line?

There are lots of metrics available to make educated opinions. Most people make the mistake of trying to compete in a minuscule segment that is overpopulated, such as the over $100 per bottle wine straight off the bat, or compete with the big boys that already have economies of scale. Pick a niche, market to an area you have interests in or natural connections to and try not to grow too fast.

Do you think there are any benefits to private label wines for the winemaker or the private labeler?

From a business point of view it's a niche market. The margins tend to be slim and you are building value in somebody else's brand not your own.

What about tips for those who just want to drink and taste wine?

Like what you like now. Your palate will change over time anyway.

Santiago Achaval

GENDER: Male

COMPANY NAME: The Farm Winery

WEBSITE: Thefarmwinery.com.com

YEAR COMPANY FORMALLY ESTABLISHED: 2009

The Farm™ Winery
cardinal
Cabernet Sauvignon

2012 Paso Robles
Adelaida District

270 cases produced

Apparently you love wine, what started the love affair?

Walking the vineyards and cellars of Napa and Sonoma during weekends in the late 80s. I was attending Stanford Graduate School of Business at the time. What attracted me most was how tied wine is to human history and psyche.

How long have you been interested in wine?

Since 1988. It was then that I knew that wine would be relevant to my life, and it was then that I formed the purpose of founding a winery.

Was there anything from history, recent or ancient, that also drew you to the field?

It was the other way around; once drawn into wine, I began to appreciate how relevant wine has been to human history. To husbandry, to survival during long winters. To celebration and the relaxing and unwinding. To the sharing of human bonds.

What was the point of starting your own wine label?

After business school I spent some time, first fulfilling the contract with the company that had financed the MBA, and then building up the amount of money I thought I would need. So it was 1998 before I took the first steps of starting my own Argentine label. It would be another 10 years before my friends Jim and Azmina Madsen invited me to start a winery in Paso Robles – The Farm Winery.

Is wine a luxury item?

Some can be. But most are not. Wine is part and parcel of the human condition and the human life. Even a very expensive wine, if enjoyed for what it is, instead of being enjoyed as a status symbol, can be considered "not luxury." I think luxury as a category comes when you start not opening the bottles.......

How did you go about starting the company from a small business standpoint?

This answer refers to The Farm Winery: My friend Jim is the most fantastic researcher. We talked about canvassing vineyards in the Westside Paso (Adelaida District AVA). And lo, he had a list of 20 vineyards for us to visit. He took charge also of all the regulatory aspects. So you could say that in fact I've only brought my expertise to the table and he's done all the founding work.

What were some of the most important steps?

Choosing the vineyards. Building the relationship with the growers so that they would be willing to farm according to our sometimes very detailed policies (which involve much more than the "normal" level of farming). Finding a place to make the wines! We're fully licensed, and operate under an AP (alternating proprietorship). Funding the capex and working capital.

What were some of the biggest challenges?

> The commute. I live in Argentina. So the travel to Paso Robles can be challenging....... Managing from afar. Trying to develop a set of procedures that allows that distance without the wines suffering for it. From my partners' point of view, I think the regulatory burden.

Did you find any aspect of setting up the company to be actually fun?

> Learning the making of the wines according to the vineyards' personality and inclination. That is, developing the founding wine philosophy and "ideology" of the newborn winery.

What appeals to you about the business?

> I love every aspect of making the wine. I even love the marketing aspects that involve sharing the wines and communicating them to the public. The feedback is very refreshing and helps us during the long development times typical of a winery.

What inspired the company name?

We believe that wine is defined by the vineyards. Not by the winemaker's personality. Not by the desire for scores. By the vineyards. And the only way to influence those vines towards a higher goal is to farm them in such a way that the vines will enjoy the results of the changes. We believe that balanced, low yields are critical to complexity and concentration. Also to the ability of the plant to express terroir.

All this is a long way to say that The Farm Winery name is because of our core beliefs about wine. When asked, "what's the secret of great winemaking?" we observe that it's 90% farming, 2% inspiration, and the balance, what others think of as 'winemaking', we say is 'mistake avoidance!'

How did you come up with your logo and labels?

Mostly the work of founder, Azmina Madsen!

So you've got the business set up and then you have to figure out which products you will sell first. Some winemakers decide this before they even start their company. Which did you do?

We decided which wines we liked and kept those vineyards. Then we started blending and finding within the barrels the wines that were hidden there. It's like sculpture! Only then we had a set of wines

How do you go about developing your blends or vintages?

> We taste. We try to think what could go with what else. We try to feel what wants to be on its own. We try and try and try again. Sometimes we get lucky: Sometimes it's evident from the grapes what the destiny of a vintage will be!

Where did you learn to develop a vintage?

> My mentor was Roberto Cipresso, Italian winemaker. He taught me to enhance my senses and find what's hidden in the flavors. Also to understand the vineyard, its cycles and its needs.

What are some key ingredients and tools that you must have?

> Great grapes from great vineyards. A nice sorting table set up around a good destemmer to make sure nothing but the good grapes go to fermentation. Some small tanks. I like stainless tanks for the ability to pump-over, but will ferment in bins if forced to. Just normal flexible impeller pumps for pumpover. A nice Moyno or peristaltic pump for older wine. A good basket press. I think I didn't actually leave anything out!! I want all the toys.

Do you need someone to help you when you develop a vintage?

When the winery as a whole is a team of people, it helps that all participate. But it's not a sine qua non.

What do you advise people to avoid when developing a wine label or vintage themselves?

Start small and stay small until you have more demand than wine. Think about sales before you think about making the wine. Define your identity before starting to make the wines. And have the wines respond to that identity. Develop the stories that will be told. They all have to be true, but cannot be left to chance.

So what do you want the buyer to come away with after tastings your creations?

A sense of joy. A recognition of us as a group of real people making real wine, not just somebody forgettable.

What are some of your favorite brands of wine?

Achaval-Ferrer and Matervini from Argentina! (actually my brand's from there, so under the rules, can't choose those…)

Favorite winemaker?

Roberto Cipresso from Montalcino.

Favorite food?

Don't have one! My problem is that I like everything too much!

Favorite beer or spirit?

Nah.... I love the quafability of beer, but can't name names. I don't drink spirits. If I did, single-malt Scotch – Laphroaig.

Favorite dessert?

Cheese!

What makes a winemaker different than or similar to other artisans such as chocolatiers, chefs, or fashion designers?

A winemaker is more a custodian and a teacher to the vineyards than an artisan. We should interpret, not make.

When it comes to terroir and how it affects the wine, do you consider yourself a floral person, a musk person, a citrus person, a woodsy person, an earthy person, or something else ?

> A Mineral Person!

Are there any developments in the field that you find very exciting?

> The return to freshness and drinkability instead of punch-you-in-the-face power.

Has the internet helped?

> Yes

Do you have advice for anyone wanting to get in the business?

> Make sure that you love wine and love making wine, and love the long hours and work of making wine. Make sure you'll be able to sell the wine!

Do you have any advice on how they can make sure they have a profitable bottom line?

Work hard, spend little, make great wines, and sell them at a high price point.

What about tips for those who just want to drink and taste wine?

Enjoy the huge diversity of the world of wine. Explore. Do your homework. Know the regions, and the producers and all those elements that make wine more than just a beverage.

APPENDIX: Dlynn Proctor

ONE OF THE BEST SOMMELIERS IN AMERICA, PLUS A WINE FILM STAR

DLynn Proctor is a man on a very unique mission. That mission is to educate the world about some of the greatest wines available.

A born and raised native of Dallas, he is now an international fixture in the wine industry. In 2008, Wine & Spirits Magazine named DLynn the "Best New Sommelier in America." This proclamation was followed by articles and features in national media such as Wine Spectator, Everyday with Rachael Ray, Decanter, and The New York Times.

His professional credentials are quite impressive. DLynn is a member of numerous organizations, including the Guild of Sommeliers, the Chaine des Rotisseurs, and the American Sommelier Association. Recently, in March 2013 DLynn was named Winemaking Ambassador at Penfolds Wine of Australia.

DLynn is recently starred in the widely acclaimed wine documentary, "SOMM". In the film, director Jason Wise follows four sommeliers as they prepare to pass the final stages of the difficult and prestigious Master Sommelier Exam. Forbes Magazine refers to this three-year Exam as the "World's Toughest Test." In fact, even allowing for multiple attempts, only 200 people have actually ever passed it.

We had a chance to speak with DLynn during his whirlwind schedule, and to find out more about what he is doing, what wines excite him, and about his partnership with Penfolds.

PRIMER: Hi DLynn, what title do you prefer we use? Master Sommelier or Mr. Ambassador?

DLYNN PROCTOR: I would have to say I like the title Mr. Ambassador, since I am not a MS yet, only an MS Candidate!

PRIMER: When did you discover your love of fine wine?

DP: I was in a fortunate position early on, being around many great collectors and enthusiasts. My tastes where almost fashioned to fine wine. So of course, I took a very keen interest in the best.

PRIMER: How do you define "fine wine" versus "regular wine"?

DP: That's a tough question. Because does fine wine mean expensive, or an affordable bottling from a storied domaine or chateau? Or does regular wine mean something that is $12.99 and cheerful? All wine, if made in a standard way, is regular. Don't get me wrong - there are fine wines that exist based on the cost of the vineyards, vines, oak, and individual handling they receive, but we can also "create" a fine wine with scarcity and demand.

PRIMER: You are the Wine Ambassador for Penfolds. They are a very old company, and are based in Australia. You are from Texas. How did you two get together?

DP: I put on a lot of back vintage Penfolds' "Grange" dinners in Texas and was always keen on the winery. I appreciated the history, heritage and mastery. Former Americas' Ambassador and Director of Education and Sales, Matthew

J Lane, and I talked for about a year before anything ever happened. Then I said yes to a position under him, and he's groomed me ever since.

PRIMER: What is your role as Penfolds' Wine Ambassador?

DP: I simply inspire. I inspire individuals, whether collector, buyer, sommelier, retailer, or novice to get excited about the wines. Through telling of the history, taking them on a scenic journey through education, and of course tasting the wines from soup to nuts. It's really exciting to taste wines that have been in production since the 50's, and also ones that have wines blended in them from 1915!

PRIMER: Does this include you tasting a lot of Penfolds?

DP: Absolutely. I have had just about every vintage of Grange, save the extremely rare ones. Most vintages of 707 and 389. All vintages of RWT, and I am working on all vintages of Magill, St Henri, and Yattarna.

PRIMER: Do you think you might consult on some future Penfolds vintages?

DP: I've spent a bit of the time in the cellar with the team, and I definitely look forward to 2014 and beyond. You have to do it to know it.

PRIMER: Since you travel a lot, what have been some of your most memorable Penfolds events?

DP: Every single one - whether the Rewards of Patience

in New York, various Recorking Clinics around the US and Canada, or the personal intimate dinners with enthusiasts and collectors.

PRIMER: Focusing on North American wine, which region do you currently find most exciting in California (or for that matter, in the US)?

DP: I'm excited about wines from the Santa Barbara area. It's quite the trend, and for good reason, to drink these balanced and elegant wines from Santa Maria, Ynez, and Happy Canyon.

Washington is also doing fabulous wines in Walla Walla and Yakima Valley.

PRIMER: Some of the Australian and Californian wines have alcohol contents of 14-16%, whereas many French wines are around 12-13.5%. Do you think this makes French wines seem more subtle?

DP: Well, a couple of things, and I'll save global warming for another 10 hour discussion. Many French and Italian wines are creeping up in alcohol and have been for years. There are regions, that by law, have higher minimum alcohol levels. It's very easy to pick on the New World and talk 'ripeness', but it is all about the producer finding balance. A word I eluded to earlier. Penfolds happens to be very elegantly balanced.

PRIMER: OK, DLynn. From military to wine guru to movie star. How did feel about being in the SOMM movie? It was a pretty grueling process it appears. Did you enjoy it?

DP: It is an incredibly grueling process, and I immensely enjoyed the making of it. Just going through it with true friends, and experiencing all of the joys and pitfalls that come with it will hopefully inspire many. Many have emailed me, messaged me or found some way to contact me to say thank you or tell me what an inspiration I had been.

PRIMER: Are you finding that people recognize you on the street?

DP: Yes! Pretty crazy. Not sure if I'll ever say, "I'm used to it." But I always engage whomever it is that says hello.

PRIMER: Is there a "wine groupie" effect from having been in the film? Any autograph seekers?

DP: Oh yes. We make fun of wine groupies - in a friendly way of course. It's pretty funny actually. I think in a way, we have all been wine groupies, because when you are younger and less seasoned and around an esteemed group, you find a way to be around them to learn as much as you can.

PRIMER: So, are there any tips you have for our readers when they are buying or tasting wine?

DP: My first tip for buying wines is to have a budget! When you have a budget, you can then seek certain regions or styles that have piqued your interest or that you have tasted before.

Secondly, find a wine gal/guy that you trust, who can help you build. They make the job easy by doing it for you. And you get to taste more along the way.

Lastly, when you do find what you like, buy smart. Buy a couple cases of each, so that you can have one bottle a month, to see how it develops over the year. That other case can age as long as you want it to. Trust me, we drink a lot more wine than we think. So buying a couple cases of multiple wines will not last as long as you think throughout the year.

That's why it is good to have the backup!

This interview originally published in the SEPIA REPORT

INDEX

COMPANY NAME: Rock Wall Wine Company — 6

COMPANY NAME: Cass Winery — 22

COMPANY NAME: Glamma Wine — 34

COMPANY NAME: Passaggio Wines — 46

COMPANY NAME: Rosa d'Oro Vineyards — 58

COMPANY NAME: Turiya Wines — 76

COMPANY NAME: Twisted Roots Winery — 94

COMPANY NAME: AH Wines — 110

COMPANY NAME: Miner Family Winery — 126

COMPANY NAME: Peachy Canyon Winery — 136

COMPANY NAME: Truchard Vineyards — 150

COMPANY NAME: Dutton-Goldfield Winery — 164

COMPANY NAME: Brecon Estate — 176

COMPANY NAME: The Farm Winery — 192

Made in the USA
Middletown, DE
05 August 2016